SEDDON ATKINSON *at work:*

400, 401 & 4-11

Patrick W Dyer

Old Pond
PUBLISHING LTD

ACKNOWLEDGEMENTS

My grateful thanks to the following for their help and support: Richard Grey, Adrian Cypher, Marcus Lester, David Wakefield, Henry Dilloway, Sam Virgo-Brown, Del Roll, John W Henderson, all at Old Pond, and of course, Linda and Jess Dyer.

ABOUT THE AUTHOR

Patrick Dyer, born in 1968, grew up during one of the most notable and exciting periods of development for heavy trucks and also the last of the real glory days for trucking as an industry. This is reflected in his subject matter. His previous books covered the LB110, 111, 140 and 141 from Scania, the 2800, 3300 and 3600 from DAF, the Ford Transcontinental and the F88 and F89 from Volvo.

Although Patrick's day job is in motor sports, he holds a Class One licence and drives whenever the opportunity arises. He is also the proud owner of a 1983 Volvo F12, finished in the livery of Edwin Shirley Trucking, which he restored with the help of long-term friend, Ashley Pearce.

DECLARATION

There were at least six recognised methods of measuring engine output for trucks during the period covered by this book. Manufacturers and magazines often quoted different outputs for the same engine using BS.Au, SAE, DIN and ISO systems, some gross and some net, much to everyone's confusion. Therefore, for clarity, only the figures quoted by Seddon Atkinson at the time are used throughout this work.

DEDICATION

This book is dedicated to all those individuals, but particularly Adrian, Marcus and David, who, through the lenses of their cameras, recorded the trucks of the seventies and eighties while working. By following their passion, these unwitting historians have made my books possible.

ISBN 978-1-908397-43-0

A catalogue record for this book is available from the British Library

Published by
Old Pond Publishing Ltd
Dencora Business Centre,
36 White House Road
Ipswich IP1 5LT
United Kingdom

www.oldpond.com

Front cover photograph
Les Baston's remarkable 400 makes a fine sight as it forges north on the A1 near Alnwick with 25,800 kg of oilseed rape in 2010, not bad for a thirty-year-old truck. *(Photo: Peter Rule)*

Back cover photograph
Seddon Atkinson designed the 400 with easy compliance to petroleum regulations in mind and the resulting take-up by the oil companies was very good for business. Conoco were among the early users, which included the big three: Shell, Esso and BP. *(Photo: Author)*

Cover design and book layout by Liz Whatling
Printed and bound in China

Contents

Foreword

By George Bennett
Editor, Truck magazine 1987-89 & 1990-97

It's a particular pleasure to introduce the latest in Patrick's excellent series of books on classic trucks because the first truck I drove as a professional, in 1973, was an Mk 1 Atkinson belonging to A M Walker of Cosby, and the first new tractor unit I was given, three years later, was a Seddon Atkinson 400. Before being assigned to the Mk 1 I'd spent two weeks of on-the-job training in a Borderer, so I know from experience that the step represented by the 400 was astonishing.

By the time it reached the market, I was driving for a small family haulage firm, John Williams of Porthmadog, in North Wales, whose tractor unit line-up consisted of two ERFs – an LV and an A Series – and a Scammell Crusader. When it came to choosing a new unit, Williams brought in a number of demonstrators, but finally chose a Seddon Atkinson 400. I was disappointed that it was day-cabbed, though I hadn't really expected anything different in such a traditional firm, but in other respects I was delighted. The Seddon Atki was considerably more stylish than the Foden I'd tried for a week, and its cab was more spacious than the new ERF B Series that had followed it. All three had had the same driveline, a 250 Cummins matched to a nine-speed Fuller gearbox, and this represented a real step up in performance compared with the 220 Rolls in the Crusader I'd been driving before.

Two-fifty horsepower sounds puny by modern standards, but it was impressive in an era when 180 Gardners were still powering mainstream 32-tonners. In an early trip in the Seddon Atki I found myself back-loading from unfamiliar territory to the east of the Peak District, and sought the advice of some local drivers about the best route home. Their response was to ask what engine was under the cab. When I replied it was a 250

Cummins they were impressed, and suggested that I might as well take the tougher route over the Derbyshire hills, rather than skirt them to the south.

The 400 turned heads, too. The first time I used it for a delivery to London, a number of drivers and forklift operators crowded round, and lined up to inspect (and approve) the cab interior. And, as Patrick suggests, the steel cab was a reassuring alternative to the fibreglass alternatives still offered by rival ERF. I was particularly aware of this because one of my former colleagues at Walker's had been killed when a steel coil crushed the ash-framed cab of his Borderer. The 400's steel cab was well put together and had virtues that were beyond the imagination of a Borderer driver – a low, flat-topped engine cover, a decent heating system, comfortable Cox suspension seat and wind-down windows. On the road, the nine-speed Fuller gearbox was much more driver-friendly than the Atki's six-speed David Brown.

From a fitter's point of view, the biggest improvement in the 400 was its hydraulically operated tilting cab. This was particularly true at Williams, where all our existing tractor units had fixed cabs and correspondingly awkward access to the engine. In fact the hydraulic pump was such a novelty that I hadn't a clue how to use it. The first time we needed to tilt the cab I rushed to operate the hand-cranked pump, but after a minute or two of energetic work, the cab remained stubbornly stationary. I continued to crank until a hose gave way with a bang, and hydraulic fluid flooded onto the ground. In my enthusiasm I'd forgotten to pull the cab-lock control before attempting to tilt the cab, and I spent the next couple of hours getting a new armoured hose from a local supplier. It was a mistake I didn't make twice.

But for all its considerable virtues, and although the 400 stood out among British trucks, it never earned a reputation to rival that of Volvo or Scania, which had muscled into the market in an era when the Borderer was still the best that Atkinson could offer, and had set a standard that most British manufacturers strove in vain to match. After all, by the time Seddon Atkinson launched the much-improved 401, Volvo had ditched the legendary F88 and replaced it with the F10, once again moving the goalposts.

When I drove for Cadwallader in the late 1970s, the company had a number of Seddon Atkinson 400s among a continental fleet dominated by Volvos. These Seddon Atkis were sleepers, of course, and were powered by 290 and even 320 Cummins, as I recall. That gave them impressive performance, but they were never greatly loved by their drivers. I remember a group of us comparing notes as we waited for customs clearance at Aosta, just south of the Mont Blanc tunnel. A Seddon Atki driver complained about its inferior ride compared with a Volvo, and he particularly criticised the in-cab noise levels. 'Ah,' said one of our colleagues, 'but I bet you wind down the window and listen to the engine when you're going through the tunnel.' Somewhat sheepishly the driver admitted that he did enjoy listening to the roar of the Cummins reverberating from the tunnel walls, but still insisted he'd prefer a Volvo. In truth, however, it was more a question of image than reality, for the Seddon Atkinson cab was considerably more spacious than the Volvo F88s, and at least as roomy as the F10 that replaced it.

The 400/401 and its smaller stablemates gave Seddon Atkinson what was probably the best chance for a small British manufacturer to survive, but foreign ownership, first by International and later by the Spanish company ENASA, proved to be no guarantee of survival in the long term. Seddon Atkinson shared the fate of fellow independents ERF and Foden, which used the same bought-in driveline options, even though the 400 cab was superior in both design and construction. All three were absorbed by larger international companies, which were initially attracted to the small British firms either to give a foothold in Europe – which didn't work for either International or Foden's owner, Paccar – or to boost their share of the important UK truck market.

Even with foreign owners, none of these small British outfits could afford the cost of developing their own competitive cabs in the 1980s, when even much larger companies such as DAF and ENASA had to cooperate with each other to build the Cabtec cab. At Seddon Atkinson, the Cabtec design replaced the latest version of the original 400 cab, and Seddon Atkinson vehicles began to lose their distinctive identity. As Enasa became absorbed into Iveco it was only a matter of time before industrial and commercial logic put an end to the Lancashire company as a separate entity.

Seddon Atkinson's fate was ultimately shared, in some form or other, by every British truck manufacturer, but back in the 1970s, the 400 series looked, and was, the best attempt in Britain to beat the Europeans at their own game. When I was given a new 400 to drive, I couldn't have been happier – if it only it had had a sleeper.

GEORGE BENNETT

Seddon and Atkinson – A brief history

The story of Seddon as a producer of trucks started with the demobilisation of Herbert Seddon from the Royal Flying Corps following the First World War. Herbert identified a need for motorised transport of goods in post-war Britain and quickly earned a reputation as a buyer and seller of vehicles. An early alliance with Ernest Foster saw the pair embark on the excursions market, a healthy and expanding sector, with a second-hand charabanc. The business, though seasonal, grew quickly and soon included Herbert's brother, Robert, too. The charabanc fleet eventually numbered 18 and, as the rear bodywork was removable, general haulage was also undertaken with the same vehicles.

Foster and Seddon, as the business was now called, grew further with distributorships for Commer, Morris and Lancia and from the late 1920s. With new vehicles hard to come by due to the depression, the company was also doing a steady trade in refurbishing second-hand trucks, often to a better-than-new standard, from the company's garage base in Salford.

All these revenue streams allowed Herbert to pursue the long-held ambition of producing his own vehicle. Legislation at the time dictated a 20 mph speed restriction for a goods vehicle with an unladen weight of over 2.5 tons; a design under that weight could operate at 30 mph and Herbert knew this would make an attractive proposition to most hauliers.

The resulting truck – a four-wheeled six-tonner – was unveiled late in 1938 with customer deliveries commencing just before the end of the year. Powered by an economical Perkins diesel engine, the truck, fully fitted out with bodywork, tipped the scales comfortably within the 2.5 ton limit. To say that it was well received would be an understatement and with its arrival the Seddon name became synonymous with innovative truck manufacturing.

Following the Second World War, production of the six-tonner resumed and the type was developed and adapted as a truck and bus chassis over the years, culminating in the Mk 5 of 1947: a model so successful it would stay in production – in one form or another – for 15 years. Seddon also enjoyed export success in this post-war period with orders from all over the globe.

Through the 1950s the company developed both lighter-weight chassis to service the distribution market below the 6-ton Mk 5 and, more importantly, increasingly heavier ones to exploit the top end of the market up to 24 tons. The latter six- and eight-wheeler sector was the domain of established companies such as ERF, Foden and Atkinson, but Seddon's renowned engineering prowess and keen pricing allowed them to develop competitive products against these giants.

After nearly becoming a victim of its own success when the company struggled to meet demand and manage stock and quality, Seddon entered the 1960s with new vigour and new ideas.

Early in the decade when it was still pursuing higher weights, Seddon rationalised its range, introduced new nomenclature and, in a bold move, axed its eight-legger chassis to concentrate on tractor units for top-weight applications. Insider knowledge, remarkable vision or sheer good luck meant that the latter decision would prove invaluable when eight-wheelers failed to gain any weight increase allowance in the changes made to Construction and Use Regulations in 1964, the government clearly favouring articulated trucks for Britain's changing haulage sector. Seddon's first premium tractor unit was the 30-4, which under the new numbering system meant a 30 ton gross capability from a four-wheel chassis. The 30-4 was available with AEC or Gardner power, a David Brown gearbox and featured a fibreglass cab produced by Seddon's own coach works, Pennine Coach Craft. Development of top-weight tractors continued through the decade and into the 1970s with the 32-4 and 34-4. From the mid-1960s Seddon tractors were equipped with a raised version of the Motor Panels' 'Supa-Cab', which Seddon had standardised on for its lighter chassis some time earlier. Although still a fixed design, the 'Supa-Cab' was of steel construction, representing a marked improvement over the fibreglass offering, and was also available as a sleeper.

By the early 1970s, Seddon's cheap, light and reliable no-nonsense trucks had won the company a loyal following which left it in a strong financial position and capable of the takeover and rescue of another of Britain's great truck producing names, Atkinson.

Although a company much like Seddon – i.e. propelled to greatness largely by the vision of one man – Atkinson's route was a markedly different one. Edward Atkinson was born in 1875 and, via an apprenticeship, became an engineer and millwright, a useful profession that was in high demand throughout industrialised Lancashire. However, being employed by other people did not meet with Edward's aspirations and in 1907 he set up in business with his brother, Harry. The repair and maintenance of steam engines became a speciality of the new company, Atkinson & Co, and it was soon granted the agency for the repair of steam wagons produced by Alley and McLellan, a Glasgow-based company more commonly known now by its later name of Sentinel. By 1916 Atkinson & Co had produced its own steam wagon and it was the construction of such machines, weighing between 2.5 and 12 tons, with which the company busied itself for the next seven years or so, including uninterrupted production through the First World War. Strong demand required a move to larger premises and a new factory was built near Frenchwood to accommodate the growing workforce of around 150 people and facilitate production of 3–4 wagons a week. These were the boom years for Atkinson as a manufacturer of steam wagons; a comprehensive range, some unique engineering and very competitive pricing brought great prosperity. However, by the late 1920s the company's fortunes had been seriously reversed. Gone was the large factory. The remnants of the business, with the remaining workforce of around 20 employees, retreated to the original, small works in Kendall Street, Preston. The age of the steam wagon was over and a relatively unsuccessful attempt at locomotive production left

This 1969 Seddon 32-4 was representative of the manufacturer's top offering around the time of the merger with Atkinson. The steel cab from Motor Panels was shared with other manufacturers, including Atkinson, for some export markets, but was made distinct with Seddon's own styling applied to the front panel and grille. The type would ultimately be developed into the 34-4, which, equipped with the Rolls-Royce 220 engine, enjoyed the distinction of being one of the lightest yet most powerful trucks available for 32-ton operation. The type was keenly priced, too, which meant strong sales and it was still current when the merged company launched the 400 in 1975. Later models featured repositioned wipers at the top of the windscreen. [Photo: Seddon Atkinson Historic Archive]

Edward with only one avenue left to explore: oil-engined trucks. Sadly, Atkinson & Co could not recover in time and, having rejected a takeover bid from Foden, was declared bankrupt in 1930. The receivers sold what remained of the company, by then little more than a small repair operation, to a consortium of businessmen in 1931. For a brief time, Edward Atkinson became a director, but his untimely death in 1932 left the company once again in some uncertainty until garage owner, William Allen, was approached as a potentially interested party for a third-axle conversion agency. Atkinson had found a small foothold in this market, which, much like the booming tag-axle industry that sprung up in the wake of the 38-tonne legislation in the 1980s, saw many four-wheel trucks converted with an additional axle to operate at higher weights. Allen liked what he saw, bought the firm outright and wrote off its debts. Atkinson Lorries Ltd emerged once again as an independent company.

Allen, with his 'new broom' philosophy, turned the company around and Atkinson produced a small profit in its first year and was soon looking for a new site within Preston to handle growth. Truck production began in 1935 with four- and six-wheel chassis covering the 7–12 ton sectors. All were powered by Gardner engines, which marked the beginning of an enduring relationship for both companies, and were marked out by a handsome cab with a distinct radiator bearing the Atkinson name at the top and, from 1937, a distinct 'A' in a circle in its centre. An eight-wheeler was available from 1937 and by the outbreak of war in 1939 Atkinson had built 50 trucks.

Atkinson's product at the time of the merger was somewhat different to that of Seddon and was, quite literally, of another era. Archaic fibreglass cabs with cramped interiors and appalling access via tiny doors placed inconveniently over the rear of the front wheels had changed little since the 1950s. However, the types were incredibly popular, enjoying a loyal following from operators, and had formed the backbone of UK haulage for a long time.
The Mark 2 Silver Knight at the back of this photograph was a 6x2 rear-steer tractor, which was originally supplied to Northern Ireland Trailers. The Ferrymasters' unit was probably a Borderer, judging by its 1970 registration, but as the nameplate is covered by a rolled-up radiator muff, it is not possible to positively identify it. (Photo: Seddon Atkinson Historic Archive)

After the war, Allen and his board decided to go for expansion rather than return to the niche-market position it had occupied before the war. As a result, by 1947 the company was re-homed in its own purpose-built factory in Walton-le-Dale and was poised for an all out assault on the heavy truck sector in the 1950s. Over the next 20 years the company went from strength to strength producing top-weight trucks bearing evocative names such as 'Silver Knight'. An ever-expanding export market spurred satellite plants to be established in Australia, South Africa and New Zealand. Like Seddon, Atkinson also switched priority to the development of tractor units and installed a separate line for assembly. However, unlike Seddon, it retained eight-wheeler production, though chassis were aimed more at tipper and bulk operators than general hauliers. By the late 1960s Atkinson was in great shape and was approaching the new decade with full order books and high expectations. However, the post-war boom had necessitated the company to float in 1948 and in 1970 ERF made a bold takeover bid which valued Atkinson at £2.8 m. A battle royal broke out between ERF and Foden with each outbidding the other in a protracted fight that raged over the summer. Leyland, with a 20 percent holding in Atkinson,

remained quiet while hauliers loyal to the company and product secured as many shares as possible. Late in October 1970, Seddon entered the fray with a new bid, which valued Atkinson at £4.8 m. Significantly, Leyland backed the bid from the newcomer and with that the cards started to tumble for Atkinson and the takeover by Seddon became inevitable.

Major restructuring followed with both companies axing loss-making ventures, such as Atkinson's operation in South Africa. Also, although each company continued to produce its own trucks, a large amount of shared engineering between the products saw the economy of scale increase, which gave the new company a stronger negotiating position with its suppliers. With this kind of rationalisation in place, work was started on the development of a new steel cab with which to take the fight to the continentals in the heavy truck sector. The cab, a modular design ultimately adaptable for use in other weight categories, would emerge in 1975 as the crowning glory of the 400 series. By that time Seddon Atkinson was under the ownership of the US giant International Harvester (IH); however, as the 400 was already in existence it can undoubtedly be viewed as the best response by a British manufacturer to the foreign invasion from Volvo and Scania.

The 400
When two become one

Dynamically, the trucks of Seddon and Atkinson had always been very good; offering well-engineered chassis that delivered good performance and reliability at a fair price, making them very attractive to operators. What the designs lacked was driver comfort and desirability, which only really became an issue when Volvo turned the industry on its head with the launch of the F88 in 1965. Until then it had been a fairly level playing field. Luckily, the new company of Seddon Atkinson realised this and, with the benefit of their combined resources, set about developing a solution. Seddon had been using a steel cab supplied by Motor Panels of Coventry for some time,

These two views of the advanced prototype 400 show just how close to the final production version the engineers had come by this point. The biggest difference on the chassis was the unusual air filter arrangement on the nearside, which consisted of a narrow, rectangular housing with two distinct downward facing vents. This was changed for production to a large, round canister mounted under the cab above the nearside front wheel.

As for the cab, apart from detail changes, the main difference was the grille, which evolved along the lines seen here, and the small vents above the rear windows, which were deleted for production. This prototype was intended to represent a 38-ton capable truck for continental haulage. As such, it was fitted with the big NTC-335 from Cummins with a lusty output of 328 bhp. This engine was listed from 1975 as one of three Cummins alternatives for the export version of the 400, but was never offered to UK customers. Those wanting that sort of power in a UK Seddon Atkinson had to wait until the 401 received the Super E320 some ten years later. (Photos: Seddon Atkinson Historic Archive)

Seddon Atkinson came up with a clever modular design that not only provided the high datum sleeper and day cab versions for the 400, but which would also allow the main pressings to be utilised for smaller cabs to suit the middle- and light-weight truck ranges that Seddon Atkinson planned to introduce in the future.

The remarkable 400 series caused quite a stir when it made its first public appearance at the Amsterdam show in February 1974. Seddon Atkinson were at pains to point out that the exhibit was very much a prototype and openly invited comment from show-goers as to what could be improved, changed or

although not exclusively as it was a Motor Panels design that was readily available to other manufacturers, and understood the benefits of strength and durability as offered by a design manufactured in steel. Atkinson too, although still persevering with fibreglass cabs, had seen the light and had even experimented, albeit with limited success, with a partial steel design of their own on the Guardsman. So with steel the material of preference, the design concept was simply to be at least as good, if not better, than the continentals at providing a safe, strong, tilting cab with sleeper option that provided the best possible environment for the driver/crew. Working closely with Motor Panels,

incorporated. The following autumn at Earls Court a revised prototype, this time fitted with a twin-bunk sleeper cab, showed that Seddon Atkinson had taken on many of the suggestions and had produced a truly competent top-weight tractor unit as a result.

Production vehicles, incorporating over sixty modifications since the first prototype, started to appear in April 1975. Although the talking point was the striking cab, underneath, the ancestry of at least one part of the new company was clearly evident in a neat and straightforward ladder-type chassis made from carbon manganese steel. Being of bolted rather than riveted construction, the unit offered strength and flexibility, but with ease of production, servicing and repair in mind. The typical side frame for tractors was 7 mm thick with a 276 mm deep section and equal-length flanges top and bottom of 76 mm while heavier rigid chassis for drawbar operation were 7.9 mm thick with a section of 305 mm and flanges of 102 mm. However, frames were heavily rationalised and apart from the different engine mounts required for the various power units on offer, a high degree of interchangeability existed. Front suspension was provided by semi-elliptic, multi-leaf springs with double-acting shock absorbers. Again, to rationalise parts the same springs, of 1,422.4 mm length, were used across the entire range from tractors to eight-wheelers. At the rear, the 4x2 chassis used a seven-spring layout with four helper springs above and double-acting shock absorbers. A slipper mount at the rear allowed the main springs to shorten under load allowing the helper spring assembly to engage and offer further resistance. The double-drive bogie utilised Atkinson's familiar four-spring balance beam design as used on previous models. All suspension was now over-slung mounted and engineers opted to use forged brackets rather than welded items on the grounds of strength and reliability. Anti-roll bars were deemed unnecessary as the set-up provided stable and smooth progress with plenty of control. The front axle was Seddon Atkinson's own I beam item drop forged from alloy steel with a six-ton capacity and mounted hubs with adjustable roller bearings. Power steering was now a prerequisite feature for heavy trucks, so the 400 was fitted with a ZF box and a Plessey pump. The latter, due to the different engine options available, was driven by belts or gears and was mounted in differing locations accordingly. The power steering reservoir was positioned, along with the radiator header tank, on the frame at the rear of the cab that also provided the cab mount and locking points. Although the location for these items was somewhat old fashioned, and certainly in stark contrast to the clean designs of the continental manufacturers, they were readily to hand for the driver and did not require the cab to be tipped for daily checks.

The standard rear axle was Seddon Atkinson's own SA-13-HR, a double

reduction design with secondary reduction in the hubs and a capacity of 13,154 kg. Although an existing design, the SA-13-HR underwent significant improvement for its new role in the 400, particularly with regard to oil seals and lubrication. An air-operated differential lock was offered as an option.

Since the 400 was designed for long-haul operation, and therefore prolonged periods away from base, it was equipped with a modern fixed-cam, sliding-shoe brake layout by Girling which would require less adjustment than a wedge-type design. A Clayton Dewandre two-cylinder compressor, air- or water-cooled depending on the engine fitted, powered the triple-line system, with Westinghouse spring brake chambers on each wheel. Air was retained in three reservoirs (for tractors), which were mounted separately in locations within the chassis rails. An automatic drain valve removed moisture from the system, though periodic manual draining of the tanks was still necessary. A useful feature of the system was the use of durable nylon piping, a marked move away from steel or copper, which was colour coded for each of the three lines. The rear axle circuit incorporated a load-sensing device to proportion braking effort, which prevented the rear wheels of the tractors locking up when lightly loaded. The driver could monitor the braking system via three Smiths dials, one for each circuit, which were set in the right-hand side of the dashboard; there was also an audible warning buzzer for low pressure. The parking-brake hand control was positioned ahead of the gear lever incorporated in the plastic tray on top of the engine hump. The lever had a slightly unusual left to right operation, rather than the more normal fore/aft of competitors. An exhaust brake with a foot switch control could be specified, but only with some engine options.

Seddon Atkinson offered the 400 series with a range of engines from Cummins, Gardner and Rolls-Royce, initially covering outputs from between 180 and 290 bhp. This gave the 400 series the ability to cope with a wide range of applications from 24 to 38 tons in tractor and rigid formats. Despite the diversity in engines, power was transferred to the gearbox via the same, air-assisted Lipe Rollway clutch: the 14 LP, PT. This unit was a pull type, dry disc design with twin 14-inch plates. Constant-mesh gearboxes from Fuller or David Brown were specified on the grounds of the type's durability and compatibility with the engines that were offered. It was generally possible to mix and match drivelines on vehicles up to 250 bhp and 36 ton; thereafter, the nine-speed Fuller box mated with one of the more powerful Rolls-Royce or Cummins engines became the only choice.

Although much reworked and improved, most of the chassis and hardware of the 400 was already familiar to many Atkinson operators. What really made the new truck stand out was its remarkable new cab. The primary function of the handsome all-metal design was to insulate the driver in a working environment that was at least as good, if not superior, to that of any other manufacturer. With this in mind, the cab was mounted high on the chassis to minimise cab intrusion from the engine and was wide to allow maximum interior space. Particular attention was placed on the crash resistance of the structure. Drivers of the Volvo F88 and Scania LB110 had soon come to appreciate the feeling of security offered by a tough cab, which helped to nurture the driver appeal of the Swedish-built trucks. Driver appeal and penetration into the wider market was exactly what Seddon Atkinson was after, so it ensured the design of the 400 could meet all expected impact legislation for the next ten years. Apart from the inherent strength offered by the all-steel cage and sheet-steel panelling, the structure also incorporated crash beams below the windscreen and across the rear panel. What was not so obvious to onlookers at the time was the fact the cab was a clever modular design which allowed easy construction of sleeper/non-sleeper types from standard tooling and

which, subsequently, would also provide much of the structure and panelling for smaller versions of the cab for the planned redevelopment of Seddon Atkinson's middle- and light-weight trucks. Inside, the cab was luxuriously finished with high-grade insulation materials, carpeted engine hump and good quality, padded plastic vinyl coverings for the dashboard and doors in a warm colour combination of black and tan. Visibility was first class with a large, almost flat, windscreen and glass all around the driver, with the exception of the rear windows on the sleeper version where the apertures were fitted with insulating blanking panels instead. A Cox suspension seat, tuned to the chassis through extensive testing, provided the driver with a comfortable and easily adjustable perch while the passenger enjoyed armrests and a head restraint. In sleeper form, the cab could be fitted with one or two bunks and curtains for all windows. Detail features included reading lights in the bunks, coat hooks, a tailored travelling case, cigarette lighter and even an alarm clock. A powerful heater/de-mister and good ventilation via window-top vents – not to mention a five-way roof hatch on sleeper models – completed the picture for the crew. A service panel at the front of the cab gave ready access to the oil dipstick and filler. The grille was self-supporting on gas struts and even contained a light for use at night. For major servicing and repairs the big cab could be hydraulically tilted to 60 degrees.

Seddon Atkinson certainly put in the hours when developing the 400 and by taking note and using extensive feedback from the industry, it presented a distinct and capable British alternative to a market dominated by foreign companies.

International Harvester (IH) had tried, with little success, to market its trucks to Europe in the 1960s, even establishing assembly operations in the UK and Germany. In 1972, it bought into the ailing Dutch company, DAF. The deal was expected to bring an exchange of ideas and technologies, but quickly degenerated, through personality clashes, to the point that any collaboration was virtually impossible. So in 1974, in a deal that was expected to be mutually beneficial, IH paid £10.5 m for the share capital of Seddon Atkinson.

The design of the 400 was all but finished by that point and IH input, though very welcome, was mostly financial. However, that did not stop the American company from becoming involved in final testing and evaluation work as is evidenced by this LHD example, in the 1975 launch livery, undergoing tests in the USA. Also present was an International Paystar liberally loaded with test weights. IH's extensive development facility at Fort Wayne, Indiana included electrohydraulic actuators capable of supporting a truck and trailer combination, which could produce the bumps and shocks of a million miles of driving in a six-week period.

Note the typical US box van trailer with the tell-tale soot stains from a tractor fitted with an upright exhaust stack, much like the Paystar. *(Photo: Seddon Atkinson Historic Archive)*

The 400's interior was a revelation in 1975 and offered the driver a spacious, comfortable, quiet and safe environment in which to work. In a style approaching that of a luxury car of the time, there was no exposed metal in the dashboard, just padded plastic and vinyl in warm and calming hues of black and brown. Then there were carpet and matching seats, bunks and panelling, which all combined to give an extraordinarily complete feel to the interior. The twin-bunk layout came as standard on the sleeper version and, due to the deceptively domed aspect of the roof, offered two spacious births for driver and mate.

The dashboard was a masterpiece of ergonomic design. Nicely finished in an easy-on-the-eye black plastic, it contained all the dials and gauges in a neat symmetrical layout, divided down the middle by a set of warning lights, all of which were easily monitored through the two-spoke steering wheel.

Note the rather unusual sideways action of the hand control valve for the parking brake and the neat dial blank, with logo, in the dash.

(Photos: Seddon Atkinson Historic Archive)

Since the 400 was launched in April 1975, there were only a couple of months of the outgoing N-registrations left before the new P-registrations of 1 August appeared, which means that Waitrose supermarkets were among the first to employ the type with this example. Waitrose, part of the John Lewis partnership, serve the upper end of the market and tend to favour town-centre locations, often high streets. This brings obvious access restrictions to many of its stores. Fortunately, the 400, with its compact wheelbase and close coupling ability, suited this role perfectly.

HHM 144N is seen taking part in a round of the Truck Driver of the Year competition, something that the company actively supported as it suited its high standards in all other areas and promoted professionalism. *(Photo: Adrian Cypher)*

Atkinson brought its vast experience of building the 'classic' eight-legger to the new partnership with Seddon and the subsequent 400 8x4 chassis drew heavily on that. The type proved very popular in what was a hotly contested sector and offered operators around 20 tons of payload and 7–8 mpg depending on spec.

This Cummins 250-powered example was new to owner-driver Rex Durham in 1976. The truck was fitted with an Eaton gearbox and Rockwell axles. Rex worked the truck out of Foster Yeoman quarries on aggregate. *(Photo: Courtesy of Henry Dilloway)*

While there was a good deal of familiarity for operators with the mechanical components of the 400, the new Motor Panels cab was something new and a world away from its predecessors. Made from steel rather than fibreglass, it was bigger in all dimensions and mounted far higher. This gave the driver a superb view of the road and allowed more distance from the engine, which cut noise levels and allowed for a roomier interior. The raised nature also allowed more air to circulate around the engine, providing more moderate working temperatures for the mechanical components, which improved engine life.

This unit, belonging to Dundee haulier Harry Lawson, was powered by the NCH 250 Cummins and drove through a nine-speed Fuller gearbox. Although an early example, it is not as significant as one that was added to the fleet later in 1975. That truck was the first customer vehicle to be equipped with a factory sleeper and was delivered following its appearance, in Lawson livery, at the Scottish Show that autumn.

(Photo: Seddon Atkinson Historic Archive)

This substantial railway arch and the hefty iron structure that has just been lowered from it on to the waiting trailer, points to some post-steam era decommissioning being carried out by British Rail in this fine photograph.

T Payne's smart 4x2 400 would have been rated somewhere between 30 and 38 tons depending on specification, making it easily capable of moving this old water tank to its next destination. UK 400 tractor units were typically rated for 36-ton operation. This gave a sensible over-capacity at the 32-ton limit, which kept some performance in hand and helped longevity, but those wanting to cut it a little finer could have specified a 400 with 34-ton capacity. In all cases the improved SA-13 axle was the standard item offered. This axle was also fitted to the 4x2 rigid chassis for drawbar work and its ability to perform across such a wide weight spectrum was a key factor in the parts rationalisation process applied to the 400 range.

(Photo: Seddon Atkinson Historic Archive)

The rather striking 'dazzle' paint scheme of this early 400 certainly made the unit stand out and suited the company's product well. Seddon Atkinson received its cabs direct from Motor Panels in Coventry. They arrived in a built-up state with doors, windows and exterior fittings in place for Seddon Atkinson to carry out trimming. The cabs came in a special paint finish, applied by Motor Panels in a dip process, which was known as biscuit. It was a type of matt top finish primer that meant cabs were ready for painting by the operator. *(Photo: Marcus Lester)*

The 400 was equipped with a modern three-wiper system, which gave good coverage of the big windscreen. However, the two-speed motor had no intermittent setting and the drag of the three blades in light rain could cause the linkages to wear prematurely as the system was not that robust. Some drivers, particularly owner-operators, would limit wiper use as much as possible to alleviate the problem and found that keeping the linkages well greased helped. The two-wiper approach of this Nicholls unit could have been applied for the same reason.
Note that wiper arms have been rotated around the splines to give maximum coverage.
(Photo: Adrian Cypher)

In 1976, J H Rose was poised to purchase a new Volvo, but was persuaded to go for a Seddon Atkinson 400 instead by Ray Keedwell, for whom the company did a lot of work. Ray's reasoning was the much cheaper purchase price of the Oldham machine. NPR 474P was one of the first 400s supplied by S A Trucks of Bristol, and was delivered by then salesman, Henry Dilloway. Powered by the un-blown Cummins 250 and driving through a nine-speed Fuller gearbox to the group axle, the truck was put on long-distance work throughout the UK. Although pictured awaiting a load of tomatoes at Weymouth docks, the delivery of Cow and Gate products to Scotland was a frequent run, with return loads of chemicals destined for Nitrovit. The truck was ironically christened Mr Rusty long before the cab's reputation for tin worm was established and actually related to the character in the *Magic Roundabout* TV series. *(Photo: Adrian Cypher)*

This 400 of Creedspeed looks magnificent in this atmospheric photograph as it takes a well-earned break from a full-on TIR existence. You can almost hear the ticking and pinging as its mechanical components cool down. Despite being an early example, LHT 478P has been fitted with the later-style grille of revised pattern and badging. It was coffee cup rings on a drawing that reputedly inspired Seddon Atkinson's distinct double snail logo. Whatever its genesis, it was not universally liked and many traditionalists lamented the loss of the Atkinson big 'A'. *(Photo: Adrian Cypher)*

MacBrayne Haulage, based in Glasgow, and Caledonian MacBrayne Ferries were able to offer a unique transport service to the Hebridean Islands delivering almost everything that the islanders needed. The ferries ran from various points on the west coast, but the biggest island, Lewis, was serviced via sailings from Ullapool on Loch Broom. Since Lewis was able to accommodate larger vehicles than its smaller neighbours, it was generally Glasgow-based tractor/trailer combinations that made the run. Trailers would be delivered, usually via the company's depot in Inverness, to the ferry terminal where a shunter would take over for the ongoing journey to Stornoway.

MacBrayne favoured the Rolls-Royce 265 engine for its Seddon Atkinson 400 series tractors and also specified it for its ERF units. However, the 400 drawbar chassis was only offered with Gardner or Cummins power at the time, so this smart example broke the mould for MacBrayne.

(Photo: Seddon Atkinson Historic Archive)

This smart 400 was new to South Wales haulier, F C Brooks & Sons. Not only was it a very early example of the 400 sleeper cab, it was also the first vehicle of any make operated by Brooks to be so equipped and as such it was indicative of the changing face of UK haulage and definitely the company's flagship. The Cummins-powered unit was used on general haulage throughout the UK and is seen here loading steel lintels from the Catnic factory in Caerphilly with Fred Brooks, grandson of the founder, directing proceedings from the trailer bed.

The company, which started in 1918, now concentrates on the house-removal sector, although some small-scale, general haulage is still undertaken.

(Photo: Seddon Atkinson Historic Archive)

By the time Clarke Chapman Ltd put this 400 to work in 1976, the company had over a hundred years of experience and, after withstanding many acquisitions and mergers, had amassed a staggering diversity in its engineering abilities. However, handling equipment on a grand scale, was, and is, key to its portfolio; of particular importance are dock cranes and high-capacity gantry systems.

This tidy 400, part of the own-account fleet, was kept busy between the company's various sites and projects.

Clarke Chapman continues to prosper and is now part of Langley Holdings Plc.

Note the rear wings are made of steel and not rubber or plastic, possibly indicating that units tended to operate with dedicated trailers, making these items less vulnerable to coupling damage. *(Photo: Seddon Atkinson Historic Archive)*

If, as was the case below, the Gardner 8LXB engine was specified, it could only be fitted to tractors with a 10 ft 3 in wheelbase rather than the standard 9 ft 6 in. If fitted in the shorter wheelbase, the prodigious length of the eight-cylinder block, compared to the six-cylinder alternatives, would have created too sharp an angle on the propshaft, which would have generated severe vibration through the drive-train making the unit virtually un-driveable and causing premature failure to components.

The 8LXB engine was noted for its economy, torque, reliability and extreme smoothness. Although it had a faithful following, its high initial cost – over 30 percent more than the equivalent Cummins – limited its appeal.

Note how vulnerable the front-mounted exhaust seems in this moderate off-road situation. *(Photo: Seddon Atkinson Historic Archive)*

The 400's front grille was a neat two-piece design, which divided at the distinct line below the badge. The lower part was spring loaded and when pulled down gave access to the release catches for the larger top portion that extended to the grab handles at the base of the windscreen. The handles were cleverly designed to double as the hinging point with the hinge pin actually inserting into the horizontal handle. Once open, the upper part was suspended on two gas struts, an advanced feature for a truck in 1975, allowing checks to be made to the oil level and fuses.

This well-travelled unit of Consolidated was a long way from home when photographed in Calne, Wiltshire. *(Photo: Adrian Cypher)*

Judging by the presence of a 4-11, a model introduced late in 1986, at the left of this photograph, this venerable and well-worked 400 of W & J Riding had completed around 12 years service for the Longridge-based company. In fact, although the middle unit is slightly obscured, this image has captured the three interpretations of Seddon Atkinson's top truck offering for the 13-year period between 1975 and 1988 – the 400, 401 and 4-11.
LVT 624P has gained the last style of grille that was fitted to the 400 from 1979 until the end of production in 1981. The snail logo has been replaced with a big 'A' and Atkinson lettering has been applied. *(Photo: Marcus Lester)*

The container revolution changed the face of transport and world commerce for good. The ease of shipping goods in this manner increased international trade dramatically, which demanded more trucks and drivers. Less lucky, however, were the armies of dockers around the world who suddenly became surplus in a system that could be handled by machinery and a few skilled operators. This early straddle carrier with chain drive looks a little antiquated by today's standards, but the speed and ease of loading that it provided were marked at the time and the equivalent machine today is essentially the same. The Manchester Liners 400 was powered by the 180 bhp Gardner, making it a T30 G6XB model rated for 30-ton operation. The tractor's weight, depending on equipment, would have been in the region of 5.8 tons.

(Photo: Seddon Atkinson Historic Archive)

Essex-based Leggett Freightways was formed by brothers Graham, Colin and Harold Linney in 1960. The Leggett name came courtesy of the previous owner of the two trucks and 'A' licence, which the brothers purchased to start the company.

During the 1970s and '80s the fleet was largely made up of British-built trucks with Gardner engines, as the firm found the units both reliable and economical on its intense trunking operations.

This 400 was one of many on the fleet fitted with the Gardner 8LXB giving 240 bhp. The after-market sleeper conversion and 'Les Routiers' stickers suggest that this unit may have been among the few on the fleet that ventured onto the continent. Note the Volvo curtains in the cab. *(Photo: Adrian Cypher)*

A sight that was once common in the UK: a National Carriers 400 with short, single-axle box van trailer working under contract for Woolworths. National Carriers Ltd operated a huge distribution and trunking fleet for a variety of customers, which in the late 1970s numbered around 6,000 vehicles. It was also one of the first to adopt an active 'green' policy and jointly developed an electric-powered, urban delivery van with Chrysler (Dodge) and Chloride.

Note that not only does this example proudly display the Atkinson big 'A' on the grille, it also has the 'Seddon Diesel' badge, covering all pre-merger loyalties. *(Photo: Adrian Cypher)*

This is the photograph that the late Pat Kennett chose for the front cover of his 1978 book on Seddon Atkinson, so its inclusion in this work was de rigueur for the author, who grew up reading his books. *Seddon Atkinson* was number three in his excellent 'World Trucks' series which ran to 14 titles by 1983 and covered most of Europe's major manufacturers. Kennett was also the founding editor of *Truck* magazine in 1974 and a hard-hitting champion of road-haulage causes. Note the curtainside (Tautliner) trailer being hauled here: an early example of the type that married the ease of loading/unloading of a flatbed with the weather cover, though not the security, of a van trailer. *(Photo: Seddon Atkinson Historic Archive)*

Waldens Frozen Foods' smart, sleeper-cabbed 400 was fitted with the legendary Gardner 8LXB engine, which delivered 246 bhp. Despite the enormous length of this engine, a consequence of the eight in-line cylinder design, it fitted snugly under the Motor Panels cab in sleeper format. Seddon Atkinson had been very careful to allow for the installation of this engine in the 400's design, knowing all too well that the 'Atkinson faithful', already stung by the Seddon takeover, would have shunned the range completely if the big Gardner had not been available. As this unit was employed on national distribution, the decision to specify the expensive 8LXB was probably made because of the engine's excellent fuel economy and reliability record.

(Photo: Courtesy of Henry Dilloway)

ICI's Mond Division was responsible for the manufacture of sodium carbonate, or soda ash. The name can be traced back to Ludwig Mond, an anglicised German who had studied under Robert Bunsen. Mond settled in England in 1867 and, in partnership with John Brunner, built a chemical plant at Winnington in Cheshire. Brunner, Mond & Co was later involved in the merger that resulted in the chemical giant, ICI. Note that this particular tank is being carried on a flatbed trailer that has dedicated twist-locks built in at the appropriate points to secure the ISO space-frame in the middle. This system allowed the trailer to be used for other work; however, the company did also use proper container skeletals.

(Photo: Seddon Atkinson Historic Archive)

Ever since man has needed to move cars in numbers, a huge amount of ingenuity has been applied to the problem. Over the years, artic and trailer combinations, drawbars and even half-cab rigids have been fitted with increasingly sophisticated split-ramp systems in the pursuit of maximum capacity. Conversely, Abbey Hill opted for a rather more simple approach to service this contract, which, rather like the straightforward engineering of the 400, provided a robust and reliable solution. The 400 cab was comparatively large for this sort of work, but with nights out clearly on the cards for this Abbey Hill driver, no doubt the spacious interior was much appreciated.

(Photo: Adrian Cypher)

In 1977 this chassis would have been listed as a D16 G6XB, a drawbar chassis fitted with the 6LXB Gardner engine. The truck would have had a capacity of 16 tons solo or could have operated at 30.5-ton GTW with a trailer. Seddon Atkinson also offered the D16 C250 for drawbar work. Fitted with a more powerful Cummins engine, this chassis could operate at the legal maximum of 32 tons with a trailer, although solo running would have been restricted by law to the same 16-ton limit as the Gardner-powered chassis.

A retrofitted 401 grille has done much to freshen this truck's appearance. Even with the less powerful Gardner engine this example must have possessed a spirited performance as a solo rigid. *(Photo: Adrian Cypher)*

The ubiquitous 400 8x4 chassis became the standard for many brick and block companies in the late 1970s and early 1980s. The change in Construction and Use (C&U) Regulations in 1972 that allowed a rigid eight-wheeler to operate at 30 ton had much to do with promoting the type. As the 400 offered a sturdy platform that could mount a self-loading device while still maintaining a very good payload, it proved very popular.

This example, fitted with a Gardner 6LXB engine and a mid-mounted crane, was operated by J R Harding & Sons, but was painted in the livery of Celcon. *(Photo: Adrian Cypher)*

Nicholas Joshua Grose started his haulage business in 1950. The company was located in St Austell in the heart of Cornwall's china clay industry and grew quickly by delivering the 'white gold' to the many industries that used it in their manufacturing processes throughout the UK. By the 1970s, the company had settled at a fleet size of around 21 trucks. The company ran a strict replacement cycle of seven years per unit, which meant that three new trucks a year received the distinctive two-tone green livery. This smart 1977 unit was fitted with a 240 Gardner engine and was at least two years old when photographed.

(Photo: Marcus Lester)

J H Rose and Sons enjoyed good service from NPR 474P, despite constant failure of hub seals in the group axle, and added a second unit to its fleet in 1977. The new truck was to the same spec, including the rear axle, but was supplied by Tilbury's of Winchester. Following the purchase of a one-man tipper operation in 1978, the company's focus shifted away from general haulage and the two 400s switched to operating with bulker trailers, which, as the trucks did not have PTOs, were equipped with donkey engines for tipping. Mr Rusty and Zebedee served five and six years respectively for J H Rose and Sons. *(Photo: Adrian Cypher)*

Early publicity material suggests that the original plan for the 400 was to market tractors as Seddons and rigids as Atkinsons. While Atkinson certainly had a long history of rigid production, such a move would certainly have upset the die-hard followers of each manufacturer and was thankfully avoided. B A Rogers Ltd operated a mix of artic and rigid tippers on a lucrative turn-around basis that saw the trucks delivering coal from South Wales and returning with scrap steel. The work was dirty, hence the thick layer of coal dust that coats the chassis of this example. *(Photo: Adrian Cypher)*

Another of the B A Rogers fleet – this time an articulated tractor/trailer combination – is seen weekending in the Swindon area. Although the coal and steel work was the same as that undertaken by the company's rigid bulk tippers, the artics gave flexibility for other work with different trailers.

While it is impossible to tell what engine is under the cab of this example, it is clearly fitted with either the Eaton or Kirkstall rear axle in preference to the group SA-13 hub reduction item. This rules out the Rolls-Royce 280 as that engine was not available with either of the optional axles. Artic or rigid, when bulk-hauling coal the grime is the same. Note the interesting twin-tank installation.

(Photo: Adrian Cypher)

Originally, Seddon Atkinson offered the Gardner 6LXB or the Cummins 250 in a 16-ton, 4x2 rigid chassis for drawbar work. The unladen weight of the Cummins-engined option was marginally more than the Gardner, but in both cases the truck came in under 6.5 tons. Gardner-powered trucks developed 183.5 bhp and were rated for 30.5-ton operation, while the un-blown Cummins produced 228 bhp and could handle the full 32-ton limit allowed for drawbars at the time. David Brown gearboxes were standard in both cases, six-speed for the Gardner and eight- for the Cummins.

Note the mattress stored behind the seats of this example, perfect for a kip across the seats. *(Photo: Seddon Atkinson Historic Archive)*

Today, semi-automatic and fully automatic truck gearboxes are commonplace and grow increasingly more clever and complex with each passing year. Mercedes-Benz should probably take the credit for really promoting the concept to the mainstream and making it popular with its EPS (Electronic Power Shift) of the mid-1980s. However, before that, in the late 1970s, it was Allison and ZF that were actively trying to market automatic transmissions to the truck industry.

Seddon Atkinson already had a working knowledge of the ZF product as it was fitted in some of the company's coach chassis, so it was no surprise when it was developed for use in the 400 series. ICI were willing partners in the development, recognising the benefits that the system presented for tanker operations in terms of smooth progress and reduced wear to the entire driveline. *(Photo: Author's collection)*

The NTE engine programme was critical to Cummins and its ambitions for the UK and European markets. The company poured a huge amount of resources into the development programme, which included exhaustive back-to-back testing against a selection of rival units around a 225-mile test route. The route was carefully chosen and included motorways, main roads, towns and gradients as steep as 1 in 8. The results showed an improvement of around 15 percent – equivalent to 1 mpg over the old NTC engine – which not only brought the E290 in line with most competitors, but actually put it ahead of many. This E290 400 was put through *Commercial Motor's* test route in May 1978 and recorded an average of 7.81 mpg. By comparison, the Volvo F88 290 only managed 5.8 mpg three years earlier. However, the Volvo F10, which did the test in September 1978, managed 8.06 mpg. Note that the test 400 was fitted with an Eaton 19128 rear axle in place of the group, hub-reduction item.

(Photo: Seddon Atkinson Historic Archive)

A 6x4 chassis seems slightly over the top for a 24-ton six-wheeler, which probably spent most of its time on high street deliveries, and, although it cannot be completely ruled out, drawbar operation is unlikely, as the 6x4 chassis was not generally offered for that application. At the time, Seddon Atkinson offered this haulage/tipper chassis with Cummins 250 or Gardner 6LXB engines. Chassis weight was in the region of 7.5 tons, which, combined with the weight of the insulated body and hefty refrigeration unit, must have impacted the payload of this example operated by Bowyers.

Seen competing in the Lorry Driver of the Year competition, the truck makes an evocative sight. *(Photo: Adrian Cypher)*

Supplying Wilkinson Transport with 400 series tractor units was a major coup for Henry Dilloway's S A Trucks of Bristol. The Wilkinson fleet had previously been dominated by Scania and switching loyalties to Seddon Atkinson spoke volumes as to the abilities of the 400 range against the very competent Swedish product. The original batches of 400s supplied to Wilkinson were Gardner powered, but buying soon standardised on the Cummins E290 following its introduction in 1978. To further enhance economy Wilkinson adopted aerodynamic aids in the form of a basic roof spoiler. The Crane Fruehauf box van trailer was perfectly suited to Wilkinson's parcel service, but was also used for all other traffic.

(Photo: Courtesy of Henry Dilloway)

Ray Keedwell started his business with an old Seddon tractor unit in 1969. Over the following six years the company expanded, mostly with examples of Scania's excellent LB110, one of the 'it' trucks of the day. However, when the newly merged Seddon Atkinson partnership introduced the 400 series in 1975, Ray was suitably impressed, especially with the price, and purchased an early example fitted with a Gardner 8LXB engine. Despite problems with the gearbox, further purchases of 400s followed with Cummins 250 engines specified until the arrival of the powerful, yet frugal, E290 in 1978. WYD 122S – fleet name 'Trouble-Shooter' – was equipped with the new economy engine and made a fine combination with Keedwell's bulker trailer. Note the Cummins badges applied to the grille and locker door.

(Photo: Courtesy of Henry Dilloway)

It is hard to estimate the value of this precious load. Rescued from the Australian bush, 'Colonial' is the last known surviving example of around 500 steamers manufactured by Atkinson. Chassis number 72, it was originally exported to the other side of the world in 1918. Repatriation followed 58 years later and just 12 months' work saw it lovingly restored to this superb condition by enthusiast Tom Varley. David Meek's 400 was no less impressive, rated as it was for 80-ton operation outside the normal C and U Regulations of the day. The truck was one of the first fitted with the then new E290 Cummins and also featured an Eaton gearbox and a 13-ton rear axle. POU 762S had the perfect spec for transporting the old-timer to the Royal Bath and West Show for display on S A Trucks' stand in 1978.

(Photo: Courtesy of Henry Dilloway)

A full house for Reece Road Transport with a 200, 300 and 400, posed in front of Chepstow Castle, making an interesting study of Seddon Atkinson's modular cab system. Although modest, at around 15 trucks, the Reece fleet frequently punched above its weight, particularly in the large amount of work it carried out for Fairfield Mabey hauling long bridge sections for the Humber and Forth crossings. Other work included livestock movement, hay and straw, all types of steel, furniture and, indeed, as 'General Haulage Contractors' almost anything was undertaken. Seddon Atkinsons were dominant, but other makes operated included DAF, Volvo, Bedford and Mercedes.

Robin Reece quit road haulage to start a successful career as an hotelier and is also well known, along with his band, as a key exponent of the UK's jazz scene. *(Photo: Courtesy of Henry Dilloway)*

Despite N J Grose's preference for Seddon Atkinson trucks, other makes did get a look in with the St Austell haulier. A notable addition to the fleet was an F88 290. Michael Grose, son of the founder, considered the Volvo a superb truck, which, with its synchromesh gearbox and sparkling performance, seemed far more modern than the 400s. However, the company's geographic location in the far west of the country meant the trucks would spend many nights away from base, making the 400's spacious cab a good deal more attractive than that of the Volvo. *(Photo: Marcus Lester)*

This pair of Cummins 250-powered 400s were new to Nitrovit's Westbury depot in 1978/9 and would almost certainly have been employed on the collection of grain from the port mill at Avonmouth and the subsequent delivery of bulk animal feed to farms in the west. In the boom period of the 1970s, Avonmouth port mill handled enormous amounts of grain, around 1 million tonnes a year, which was mainly imported from the USA and Canada. However, the dairy industry contracted as a result of the introduction of milk quotas which caused a general downturn in the mid-1980s. The Nitrovit name, along with its fine livery, was one of many that were lost in the rationalisation that subsequently swept through the industry. *(Photo: Courtesy of Henry Dilloway)*

This smart 400 makes a fine combination with a very robust looking wide-axle spread fridge trailer. The unit was one of a number of 400s run by the Somerset haulier, Hopkins. Although it is not fitted with a nearside locker, it does seem to have gained a panel in the appropriate area, the original diagonal line of the cab bottom being clearly visible. As the factory did not supply such a panel it must be assumed that the owner made the modification, possibly for aesthetic reasons. The unit is also fitted with a later style of grille. *(Photo: Marcus Lester)*

SMS operated a fleet of around 26 trucks on the collection and delivery of 'skim' milk. Not to be confused with 'skimmed milk', this was the waste and top skim from the dairy farms that was not considered to be good enough for human consumption and was mostly used for pig feed. The company was started in 1958 and became Skim Milk Supplies in 1964. Cliff Cox joined the company in 1960 and eventually bought it from the founder in 1967. A fleet of Seddon and Atkinson trucks paved the way for Seddon Atkinsons following the merger, although loyalty eventually shifted to ERF for a brief time before the business – though not the name – was sold off. Chambers Engineering of Aylesbury supplied the 400 tractor units while the trailers came from Melton Tankers. Since the trailers were not carrying milk for human consumption, there was no requirement for total top access for cleaning and the driver could carry out all operations while at ground level.

One of SMS's Cummins-powered trucks clocked an astonishing 1.3 million miles with just standard servicing and could have achieved more had it not ended up in a ditch!

(Photo: Marcus Lester)

EKV 352T was one of two identical spec 400 series units purchased by Ellis Greaves to perform both general haulage and, to a lesser extent, low-loader operations. To up-rate the trucks so that they would perform well in the secondary role, they were fitted with 13-ton rear springs and 12.00x20 tubed tyres.

This increased the GVW of the units from 16 to 19 tons, which allowed for a GTW of 50 tons under STGO regulations. The heavy-duty springs also permitted the fifth wheel to be set back by 5 inches, giving the necessary trailer clearance without exceeding the maximum length.

Midland-based Ellis Greaves had previously operated Mk 2 Atkinsons. The E290-powered tractors were both supplied by Vee & Inline Diesels.

(Photo: Seddon Atkinson Historic Archive)

The 400 series was not fitted with anti-roll bars or any other stabilising equipment for that matter; indeed, springs were rationalised across the entire range for artics and rigids and the fact that the trucks rode and handled indicated a particularly well-sorted chassis. This interesting drawbar combination operated by Frigfreight looks distinctly top heavy and potentially wobbly, even standing still, with the high mounting of the bodies and hefty refrigeration equipment at the top. However, the demountable bodies were specially designed and manufactured by Ray Smith Demountables of Peterborough with a lightweight frame specifically for refrigerated vehicles.

(Photo: Seddon Atkinson Historic Archive)

Confusion reigns with this photograph depicting the same truck, somewhat later in life, but now with fixed bodywork in place of the demountable item and – according to the man who was behind the lens – no drawbar coupling to manage a trailer. Performance at 16 tons must have been startling and range, courtesy of the twin 80-gallon tanks, truly epic. A further anomaly concerns the changes to the sleeper windows and, indeed, the cab panelling below; all of which seems to hint at an after-market conversion from a day cab. But the truck was definitely fitted with a factory sleeper in the earlier photo so maybe it was re-cabbed at some point. *(Photo: Adrian Cypher)*

Bulwark had a long history of operating the products of both Seddon and Atkinson and, undeterred by the merger, purchased 400s from the start and in numbers of up to 50 a year. The usual spec was a 4x2 day cab and the engines were generally Gardner 8LXBs. Even before the takeover by Seddon, Bulwark enjoyed a close association with Atkinson. In 1964, Atkinson's Guardsman show truck was displayed in the Bulwark livery and was lined up for running trials and evaluation on the tanker fleet. However, the Guardsman's bold styling missed the mark with conservative hauliers and the Cummins V8 engine struggled to gain favour, leaving Atkinson with no option but to drop the model and concentrate on a more traditional product.

(Photos: Seddon Atkinson Historic Archive and Adrian Cypher)

Rubbing salt into the wound? The salesman responsible for selling this fine line-up of 400s to Canning Transport, right under the nose of such an established rival as Leyland Trucks, certainly scored a major coup. The irony of the latter's name appearing on the door, as part of company's address, was too good to be ignored by Seddon Atkinson's press department.

Mechanically, the Leyland Marathon was a worthy rival to the 400. Introduced two years earlier in 1973, it offered similar performance from a range of specs, but its cut-and-shut version of the Ergomatic cab, already a ten-year-old design at the time, couldn't compete with the Motor Panels offering of the 400.

Note Canning's distinct wrap-around headboard, with which it replaced the standard factory item. *(Photo: Seddon Atkinson Historic Archive)*

Richard Preston had already been running a successful agricultural business for over 20 years when he moved into road haulage in 1957. The new venture grew steadily over the next 12 years gaining a reputation for service and quality. The company's location in Potto allowed it to expand rapidly in the 1970s due to the increased industrial output from Teesside, particularly in the steel and, chemical sectors. This corresponded nicely with the introduction of the 400 series and, following good experiences with early models, the smart red fleet swelled with examples such as this.

(Photo: Marcus Lester)

In general, the 400 was not noted for having a particularly good turning circle and the situation was not improved with the addition of the second steering axle for the 8x4 chassis. In fact, the turning circle of the Volvo F86 8x4, one of the 400's most direct rivals in this sector, was tighter by ten feet. Steering input to the second axle was made via a secondary slave ram. Perhaps, by adopting a similar approach to Volvo, which relocated the steering box between the two front axles, performance in this area could have been improved on the big Seddon Atkinson.

This exceptionally smart example, with a beautifully crafted aggregate body, was new to Somerset County Council in 1978. *(Photo: Courtesy of Henry Dilloway)*

In the late 1970s, all the exciting and glamorous on/off road trucking requirements of the MOD (Ministry of Defence) were performed by a mix of types from Bedford, Foden and Scammell. However, the Seddon Atkinson 400 was purchased in large numbers to perform the essential day-to-day road transport duties that were required to keep all three services supplied and mobile. This line-up of five brand-new examples outside the Oldham plant illustrates the typical MOD spec of a 4x2, day cab tractor with Rolls-Royce engine, Fuller gearbox and group axle.

For operators, the headboard was a useful standard fitment on the 400, but although fitted here they would have been removed soon after arriving at the operating units.

Note that two of the units appear to be painted in a dark gloss finish, possibly suggesting end use by the Royal Navy?

(Photo: Seddon Atkinson Historic Archive)

Despite the introduction of the 300 series as a dedicated, three-axle, 24-ton chassis in 1978, Seddon Atkinson still offered operators the choice of the 400 in two 24-ton chassis, one with a Gardner engine and one with a Cummins, if the larger vehicle was required. Both were available in two wheelbases of 15 ft and 17 ft 6 in. The type seemed to suit agricultural environments, being big enough to mount decent-size bodies, yet still capable of negotiating narrow roads and accessing small farms. This fine example is equipped with an early-style hydraulic arm and grab to facilitate loading/unloading on isolated farms. *(Photo: Seddon Atkinson Historic Archive)*

This wonderful Gardner-powered, 30-ton tipper appears to have the shorter of the two wheelbase options of 18 ft 10 in, which, with a full tank of diesel and a spare wheel fitted, gave an unladen chassis weight of 8.1 tons – slightly less than the Cummins-powered alternative at 8.4 tons. However, both had the potential of offering a 20-ton load. Note that this truck is fitted with the 80-gallon diesel tank, when the standard fitment for rigid chassis, except drawbars, was the 40-gallon item. Both tanks had a locking cap as standard.

(Photo: Seddon Atkinson Historic Archive)

Whichever way you look at it, the 400 range was a significant improvement on the previous Atkinson products. Of the two merged firms, Atkinson was certainly the more conservative with a traditional product that had changed very little since the 1950s. Seddon had at least moved to steel cabs in the late 1960s, and, while not a tilting design, this move helped to forge a relationship with the supplier, Motor Panels, which would prove fruitful in the development of the 400.

Hammond of Sittingbourne, Kent had run Atkinsons since the days of the Borderer and continued with the merged product through the 400, 401 and 4-11 to the Strato, remaining with the marque until closure of the haulage business in the mid-1990s. A great deal of traffic was paper reels and plasterboard, but the company was equipped for most general haulage jobs with a trailer fleet that included tippers, tankers, tilts and curtainsiders alongside its usual flats. This superb line-up of Hammond 400s shows a mix of Mk 2 and Mk 3 grilles.

(Photos: Courtesy of Mark Robinson)

Post-1983 and operating at 38 tonnes with a tri-axle trailer, this 1979/80 400 looks in very good shape with no obvious 'tin worm' yet to be seen. Despite the reputation that the Motor Panels cab gained for susceptibility to rust, a thorough anti-corrosion process was in place at the Coventry plant from the outset. This included a new electrophoretic treatment. Cabs underwent a degreasing spirit wipe, an alkali spray and rinsing cycle and phosphate sludge removal before paint was applied electro-statically in a dipping tank. The process offered total coverage of the entire structure.

(Photo: David Wakefield)

Even without the Cummins grille badge fitted to this example, the presence of the big 14-litre engine is evidenced by the nearside mounting of the air stack whereas Rolls-Royce- and Gardner-powered examples had this item on the offside.

The unmistakeable John Raymond livery sits very well on this 1979/80 sleeper cab. The company ran both 250 and 290 Cummins engines in its 400 series tractor units. This one, given the long-distance implications of the sleeper cab, was probably fitted with the latter and – as a post-1978 example – this would have been the superb E290 version with improved fuel economy.

Note how rust, which has festered from stone chips, has started to take hold of the 'tin' grille even though wheel and tank condition suggests that a chassis re-paint has taken place recently. Maybe a replacement 401 grille was to be fitted. *(Photo: Marcus Lester)*

Caswell, like many of the pioneering haulage companies in the UK, started out as a horse-and-cart operation. A switch to powered vehicles was made in the 1920s and steady growth followed. Atkinson trucks, with Gardner engines, had featured in the fleet since the 1950s and by the late 1970s a number of 400s were running in the smart blue-and-red livery. Caswell continued trading until the business was wound up in the early 1990s. Note that the rear of the cab is glazed, with the normal window blanks of the sleeper version having been removed. *(Photo: Marcus Lester)*

It's a dirty job, but someone has to do it and as the saying goes: 'where there's muck, there's brass'.

Despite its role, the driver of this 400 kept the unit in a very acceptable condition. The presence of a big 'A' logo and 'Knights Head' emblems suggests a strong link with Atkinson products of old. However, the grille has also been modified on the offside to accommodate an extra Seddon Atkinson 'snail' logo, so this operator was obviously happy with the merger and combined product.

Note that an International badge has also been added. Perhaps this operator was one of the few that tried the UK-assembled Loadstar, which was available for a short time in the 1960s. *(Photo: Marcus Lester)*

Access to the historic buildings of breweries was often restricted by their locations in town centres and the original access routes designed to suit nothing bigger than the average horse-drawn cart or brewery dray. With this in mind, brewery transport was another role that suited the compact dimensions of the 400 series tractor when built with the short, 9 ft 6 in wheelbase option, especially in day-cab form because it allowed generous trailer clearance. Just visible on this Cummins-powered example is the new rear air stack arrangement introduced in 1978 which, though not a full snorkel type as favoured by European manufacturers, did pull in reasonably clean air from behind the cab. *(Photo: Adrian Cypher)*

In the spring of 1979 Cummins announced a new engine, the Turbo 250. Following in the wake of the successful 'Series-E' big cams introduced a year earlier, the Turbo 250 was something of a hybrid. Based on the old normally aspirated NHC 250, the new engine was fitted with the Holset HC3 turbocharger of the E290 and revisions were made to the manifold and injection. Although engine speed was reduced and output remained the same at around 240 bhp, torque was up by 140 lb-ft. The engine became a lugger, like the big cams, and Cummins claimed a 10 percent improvement in economy.
The beautifully executed livery of this 400 really sets it out. Latham Timber has a remarkable history as a family-run business that has been importing timber since 1757. *(Photo: Seddon Atkinson Historic Archive)*

The RAF's No 2 MT (Mechanical Transport) Company was established in 1940 and gained squadron status in 1954. Since its original wartime location of Kings College, Cambridge, the autonomous unit has had several homes. The most significant has been RAF Stafford where it was based for 48 years and then RAF Wittering, since 2006, with its handy location on the A1 just north of Peterborough. This 1980 400 with Rolls-Royce 290 was typical of the type joining the squadron around that time to replace ageing AEC Mercury and Leyland Mastiff units.

The supply of RAF bases on the continent meant frequent channel crossings were necessary and the squadron lost one of its 400 tractors when the *European Gateway* capsized, following the collision with the Speedlink *Vanguard*, in 1982. The unit, trailer and load were all recovered during the salvage operation and returned to the RAF, but were subsequently written off. Note the seldom-fitted 400 door badge. *(Photo: No 2 MT Squadron)*

Strong manufacturing areas, such as Stoke-on-Trent, demand a strong haulage sector for the movement of raw materials in and finished goods out. The relationship is, however, double edged and when manufacturing suffers so does road haulage.

Ken Beresford set up his Tunstall-based business in 1953 following a spell as depot manager for BRS in the same town. The company favoured ERF and especially liked Gardner-powered examples. However, Seddon Atkinson 400s did feature originally as they were the first to offer a proper sleeper cab.

These two examples, in the famous Beresford livery, were photographed at the Tunstall yard in the depths of winter and are covered in the salty road grime of the season. However, great importance was placed on appearance and both would have been rigorously washed before returning to the road. *(Photo: Adrian Cypher)*

The 400 was subject to constant development to improve it and rectify those faults that only surface once a new vehicle is operational. Various items were modified, including the radiator and header tank mounts, rear spring hanger brackets, fuse location and air intake position. Some operators reported fouling of trailer king-pins on the rear cross member during hitching up, so Oldham's engineers changed the design to incorporate a distinct dropped section in the middle to give the necessary clearance.

Somerset haulier, Wheelers Transport, ran a number of 400 and 401 units – both day cab and sleeper – in 4x2 and 6x2 formats. *(Photo: Marcus Lester)*

This smart 400 of Heanor Haulage highlights the height discrepancy between tractor and trailer that could lead to cross member damage.

Retrofitting a 401 grille was a cheap and easy way to freshen up the appearance of an older 400. The deception might even trick the casual observer, or even customer, into thinking a fleet was full of the later vehicles. However, the ruse rarely extended beyond the grille. Doppelgangers were easy to spot by the absence of the following when compared to a genuine 401: SMC front bumper incorporating an air dam, large aluminium cab steps, SMC front wings of a different profile, flush door handles with IH logo, different cab profile below side window of sleeper cab (and no locker option), new rear cab support and locking mechanism, up and over air stack, cylindrical aluminium diesel tank – though military 401s did retain the rectangular item – and new rear light assemblies. Closer inspection would also reveal a host of differences in the chassis and cab interior. *(Photo: Marcus Lester)*

LYB 530V was another of Keedwell's E290-powered 400s. Being a 1979 unit it was fitted with the replacement steel grille introduced that year. The new item featured stainless steel trim strips rather than the chrome ones of the previous grille and these were supplied loose for fitting after the application of the customer's livery. The truck was fitted with twin bunks and later a much larger diesel tank replaced the original item on the offside: a common modification that was made to many of Keedwell's trucks at the time to improve range.

(Photo: Courtesy of Henry Dilloway)

Beresford Transport ran a number of units in the familiar yellow, white and red colours of JCB. The trucks collected finished machines from the JCB plant in Uttoxeter and would deliver them all over Europe. Although painted in a customer's livery, the trucks were not dedicated to the work and could also, on occasion, be seen hauling Beresford's usual tilts.

In the late 1970s, the Tunstall-based company was regularly sending around 30 of its 80 strong fleet to the continent with destinations including France, Belgium, the Netherlands, Germany, Austria, Italy, Spain and Yugoslavia. *(Photo: Marcus Lester)*

The date 3 June 1984 marked the start of a remarkable relationship for Les Baston and VGR 808V, which, at the time of writing, was still going strong 28 years and 2.5 million kilometres later.

VGR 808V was new to Renner Haulage of Northumberland in 1980. It was the youngest of three 400s operated by the company and was mainly employed on bulk grain work.

Before Les put the four-year-old unit to work he undertook what he considered an essential modification to the gear stick. Aware that Seddon Atkinson had modified this on the 401, Les cut a hole in the cab floor, fabricated a bracket to mount the gear stick on top of the engine and finished the job off with a new 401 gear stick boot. This eliminated the extra linkage of the original set-up, which tightened the gate spacing and reversed the shift pattern back to a conventional one that progressed up the box from left to right. *(Photo: Les Baston)*

Ah, the halcyon days of trucking! This is how the author fondly remembers UK 32-ton operation with loads roped and sheeted on flatbed artic combinations running on four axles, and of course the sun was always shining! Although a romantic and rose-tinted view, there is no denying that the trucks of that era had much more character than their modern counterparts – and often more interesting liveries – and that methods and practices, such as roping and sheeting, were far more interesting for the observer. Almost certainly Cummins powered, Vitamealo used this example for the delivery of animal feed throughout the UK. *(Photo: Marcus Lester)*

Cumbrian cattle haulier and dealer, Keith Ewbank, switched from foreign trucks to Seddon Atkinson in 1978 with the purchase of CEC 910S and added one per year over the next two registrations. The three units were all E290 powered with Fuller 9-speed gearboxes, Rockwell R180 rear axles and ran under contract to a national wholesale meat supplier. The trucks averaged around 91,000 miles per year on a regular run between Stranraer, Penrith and Southampton carrying cattle and sheep. Fuel consumption was a major factor for Ewbank in the purchase of the first 400 and it was the fact that the Seddon Atkinsons saved around 20 gallons per round trip compared with his previous vehicles that led him to purchase further 400s for the fleet. The fitting of Uniroyal air deflectors was also found to help fuel consumption with the tall tri-axle trailers. Although running with the lower-height Parkhouse cattle container here, the third unit was to be similarly equipped in time. The trucks also featured Airdromic auto lube systems. *(Photo: Seddon Atkinson Historic Archive)*

The next significant development for VGR 808V was the addition of tag axle, which allowed Les to operate at the 38-tonne limit. Haverton Truck Engineering of Billingham carried out the work in February 1986. By this time Les had also modified the steering lock by screwing in the axle stops; this was a great improvement, though it was still not up to the standards of Volvo or Scania.

This rear view shows the radiator header tank arrangement of the 400, which was mounted on the cab support bracket. Since VGR 808V had a turbocharged engine, this was the larger of the two tanks that could be mounted in this position. Note that the unit had rear glazing and not the blank insulation panels that were usually fitted to the sleeper cab. *(Photo: Les Baston)*

By the late 1970s, the sleeper cab was really catching on with hauliers, but when the 400 range was launched in 1975 the UK industry was only just starting to come around to the idea of drivers spending nights out in their cabs. Drivers' digs, cafés equipped with sleeping accommodation and roadside trailer swapping to avoid drivers staying away from home were still rife. So, although it had developed a sleeper version from the outset, Seddon Atkinson concentrated its early 400 production on the day cab and even built common spec versions to put into stock.

The distinct double window profile of the 400 sleeper worked aesthetically when it really shouldn't have. The unique appearance was a consequence of the modular design, which allowed a range of cabs to be produced for the 400, 300 and 200 trucks from a standard set of pressings to which filler panels could be added to increase width and height. To create the sleeper, the panel behind the door, incorporating the larger window, was added. Scania had a similar modular system for its LB range. However, the extra panel used to create the LB sleeper did not incorporate a window; instead, the rear panel went around the corner and incorporated a quarter light so it did not create an odd look.

(Photo: Marcus Lester)

Seddon Atkinson and Motor Panels went to great lengths to try to protect the 400 cab against corrosion. Water traps were designed out and all welded seams were vertical to allow water to run off. New paint processes were employed and the structure was undersealed. Despite all this, it still developed something of a reputation for rust, with prone areas being the front panel, windscreen and side window surrounds and the seams above the front wings. Not all cabs suffered to the same degree. Although showing signs of age in this later photograph, YHT 2V seems to have fared quite well. Perhaps individual liveries, and the competence with which they were applied, played a part in a cab's resilience to rust Note the optional locker on the nearside rear of the cab. When fitted, this item changed the cab profile considerably. *(Photo: Marcus Lester)*

Bernard Atkins started Atkins International in 1926 and by the time this 400 was purchased it was, indeed, truly international. As well as operating on routes throughout Europe, the company was one of the first UK firms to establish a remote office in Cherbourg from where it ran French-registered trucks.

This 400 with the E290 Cummins engine worked in Atkins' mixed fleet, which included a number of Trilex-wheeled FIAT 170s. Like other 400s on the fleet, this unit probably gained a trailing axle post-1983 to cope with 38-tonne operation. Note the extended air stack and strangely angled air horns. *(Photo: Adrian Cypher)*

Les Baston, like many others, updated the look of his 400 by retrofitting the new SMC grille of the 401. Seddon Atkinson actually went to great trouble in designing the new grille so that it could, indeed, be used in this way. This was mainly because the old tin grille, which was very susceptible to stone chip damage, could rust prematurely and quite literally fall apart. However, it also gave great exposure to the Seddon Atkinson name and big 'A' logo and quite possibly gave the impression that the company was selling a lot of 401s too. For many years the SMC grille was one of the most ordered spare parts from Seddon Atkinson dealers. Les's trusty flat seems cubed out with this generous and bulky load of Nissan car parts destined for Sunderland. *(Photo: Les Baston)*

ICI ran a big fleet of tractors with the general specification of this 400. Although the Oldham range was well represented in the fleet, Seddon Atkinson did not have it all its own way. Other makes, notably Scania, were also present.

In all but its lowest-powered forms, the 400 measured up to the LB111 and *Truck* magazine actually pitched examples against each other in a three-way test with a Foden just after the launch of the 400 in 1975. The LB111 was also new at the time – having just been developed from the LB110 – and its superb DS11 engine gave it a distinct performance advantage over the other two machines. However, the Seddon Atkinson 400 that was tested was fitted with the un-blown Cummins 250 where perhaps the 290 turbo may have been a fairer match. However, the 400 was £160 cheaper than the Scania at £11,480. *(Photo: David Wakefield)*

The wonderful livery on this 400 owned by family haulage firm, Robinson, was a departure from the company's normal maroon and cream scheme, though both enjoyed the same level of detail in the finish. 'Flying Scotsman' was part of Robinson's small, mixed fleet based in Northallerton, which featured a mix of manufacturers including a number of pre-merger Seddons. General haulage with flatbed trailers was the company's core business, which it could augment with a storage capability; however, the movement of single 20 ft containers on skeletal trailers was also undertaken. *(Photo: John W Henderson)*

Production of the 400 centred on tractors, rigids for drawbar operation and the classic eight wheeler for construction/tipper work. This three-axle 6x4 chassis for 24-ton operation was not that common, the role being more suited to the 300 series introduced in 1978. The 300 was specifically designed for this weight category, but was only available with the IH engine producing around 194 bhp, a restriction that created a moderate demand for the 24-ton 400. Sheldon Jones ran a number of 400s with this configuration to supply its milling operation in Bruton, Wells. The usual spec was Gardner 6LXC engine, David Brown or Eaton gearbox and Norde rubber suspension. Dunn Spencer supplied the smart, alloy, bulk feed bodies. The company also operated the smaller 200 series, again fitted with Dunn Spencer bodies. *(Photo: Courtesy of Henry Dilloway)*

Peter Maughan's smart eight-legger cable loader obviously hadn't shifted much bulk scrap when this photograph was taken. The truck had a 6LXB Gardner engine, David Brown gearbox and Rockwell axles. Also, with the high stresses imposed on the chassis when lifting a bulk skip over the rear and the potentially high centre of gravity when loaded, Maughan thought it prudent to spec this 400 with Norde rubber suspension instead of the usual multi-leaf spring set-up. Note the cable control levers, which are angled toward the window to allow the driver to complete the loading operation without leaving the cab. *(Photo: Courtesy Henry Dilloway)*

N J Grose used this 8x4 30-ton tipper for the delivery of china clay and coal to premises that were inaccessible to the company's artics. The truck was purchased with the consecutively registered ERL 127V, a 4x2 unit. The tipper was fitted with a Gardner engine and the unit an E290 Cummins. This marked a point in the company's history where a shift towards Cummins power units became apparent. This policy was steered by Michael, the founder's son, in an effort to rationalise parts and servicing within the fleet and thus improve efficiency and profit. Note the after-market sleeper conversion fitted to this example. *(Photo: Marcus Lester)*

William Henry Grose was the brother of Nicholas Grose and operated his business from the same yard in St Austell. His smaller fleet numbered around five units for much of the time but was gradually wound down to a one-man outfit towards the end. William originally favoured ERFs, but gradually came round to Seddon Atkinson and the 400 as the benefits of rationalisation with his brother's trucks were obvious. This example, no doubt steered by his nephew, Michael, was also fitted with the E290 Cummins. Both companies were proud members of the Road Haulage Association, which was reflected in their professional approach and smart turnout. *(Photo: Marcus Lester)*

Rather than introducing different marks throughout its production, the 400 was instead subject to constant and ongoing development between 1975 and 1981. Seddon Atkinson's approach was a reactive one, fixing problems as operators and dealers highlighted them.

However, it is possible to divide up 400 production by the three grille types that were fitted, all of which are conveniently displayed here in this fine line-up of Guest 400s. The first design (far right) was fitted between 1975 and 1977, the second (middle) between 1977 and 1979 and the third between 1979 and 1981. Guest of Bath ran a large number of 400/401 units and favoured Rolls-Royce engines, generally finding the 265L well suited to its operations. *(Photo: Marcus Lester)*

FVR 664V rolled off the production line in December 1979. The 4x2 unit with E290 engine was destined for farmer and cattle dealer, Stewart Powell, of Cheshire. The truck was finished in a striking and unusual livery, which, though not obvious here, featured a wood effect for the upper half of the cab. The spec was the classic Cummins/Fuller/Rockwell combination and the truck also featured heavy-duty springs to manage the impressive trailer and its bovine loads. The double-deck, Crane Fruehauf tri-axle was fitted out by Body-Craft of Worcester and was a whopping 15 ft tall. To facilitate loading of the upper deck, the trailer was fitted with an electrohydraulic lift at the rear. *(Photo: Seddon Atkinson Historic Archive)*

Trailer clearance/length is obviously not an issue on this example, but because it offered such compact dimensions, a 400 series tractor unit, in day-cab form with the 9 ft 6 in wheelbase, could accommodate a maximum trailer length of 41 ft 3.1 in. This was only possible if the distance between the kingpin and the centre of the axle was set at 1 ft 8 in, which allowed for just over 4 ft of trailer between the kingpin and cab. This set-up would create an imposed load of 9.5 tons through the rear axle.

The messy business of hauling liquid rubber was probably the order of the day for these two 400s of Revertex. Note the padlocked battery cover of this example. *(Photo: Seddon Atkinson Historic Archive)*

The 8x4 tipper market was a hotly contested sector in the UK and the 400 did very well against stiff competition from manufacturers such as ERF, Foden, DAF, Magirus-Deutz and Volvo. Apart from the detail changes that came with the constant development of the entire 400 series – such as the grille – and changes to engines made by the respective producers, the 30-ton, eight-legger, tipper chassis remained virtually the same throughout 400 series production. Whether Cummins or Gardner powered, the chassis were available in two length variations that were measured from the centre of the front axle to the centre of the rear bogie. The variations were 18 ft 10 in and 20 ft 3 in.

Note the big 'A' logo that has been fitted to the grille by the driver of this fine example.

[Photo: Seddon Atkinson Historic Archive]

January 1989 and VGR 808V is loaded with paper reels in Blyth for delivery to Dumfries. Although it is not visible from this angle, Les has now fitted an extension pipe to the original short air stack to collect air from over the top of the cab. Seddon Atkinson, of course, did this for the 401 and Les capped the extension with the ram-air type scoop of that model. Les found that the cleaner air from above the cab substantially improved the life of air filter elements.

Nights out were a lot more comfortable, too, as VGR 808V was now fitted with a night heater. *(Photo: Les Baston)*

Only the earlier T-registered examples were fitted with the intermediate style of front grille. Certainly by the time that V-registrations came in August 1979, the third and final design for the 400 was firmly established. This John Raymond unit could have been pre-registered before the changeover, or the older style item may have been retrofitted to replace a damaged one of the correct pattern.

A number of John Raymond's 400s were fitted with the Gardner 8-cylinder engine and this one also appears to have the optional Kirkstall axle in place of the SA-13 hub-reduction item. Note the low-mounted corner wind deflectors and the additional 40-gallon tank. *(Photo: Marcus Lester)*

VGR 808V's tag-axle improved productivity greatly and gave Les the flexibility to use twin-axle trailers from rental companies or customers while still operating at 38 tonnes, and with much of his work derived from farms and building sites it could be raised to gain extra traction when necessary. However, it did have one drawback. The front wheel studs of the 400 series were susceptible to breakage in general, but Les found the frequency increased dramatically after the tag-axle was fitted. Les cured the problem by fitting a set of front spigot hubs taken from an early 401. The truck is pictured with a load of peat bales ex-Grimsby docks in 1992. *(Photo: Les Baston)*

Being producers of a specialised product, Geo L Scott & Co had no need to advertise its presence via a flashy paint job. After all, those in the market for the raw components of industrial electric motors probably knew all about the company. However, even if it does scream 'own-account user', this plain livery and subtle sign writing actually works rather well on the big Motor Panels cab of the 400. LVT 303V, a Cummins-powered unit, was, indeed, employed on the supply and delivery of the company's laminated steel products destined for electric motor production. The 1979/80 truck appears to have visited the continent in the course of its duties and the tidy condition, coach-style wheel trims and abundance of trucking stickers suggests a proud and enthusiastic driver. *(Photo: David Wakefield)*

Even ignoring the updated 401 grille, it is still hard to believe that, for a time, Seddon Atkinson offered these two alongside each other. The stratospheric jump that the company made from the timber and fibreglass construction to the steel Motor Panels cab was remarkable. The new cab offered a tilting facility, easy access, comfortable seats, noise insulation, decent heating and ventilation, integrated sleeper and superb visibility. However, what can't be denied was the good honest working ability of an old Atkinson. This example, far from being on the way to an eager preservationist, was actually off to finish its days working in an opencast quarry in Northumberland when photographed in 1995.

(Photo: Les Baston)

During the 1970s and '80s, the fleet of Welsh haulier Mansel Davies and Son was a diverse mix. Domestic products from home-grown Leyland rubbed shoulders with Anglo-American trucks from Dodge, Bedford and Seddon Atkinson. The company also ran a good number of imports, including Scania, Volvo and DAF. That the 400 was successfully operated alongside such machinery was praise indeed for its abilities.
Note the 401 grille fitted here and how the after-market headboard changes the truck's appearance when compared to the factory item. *(Photo: Marcus Lester)*

Rolls-Royce built its first diesel engine in 1949, but it was 1966 before it offered power units to truck manufacturers. However, the now-legendary Eagle range was developed from a successful line of industrial engines with a proven track record.

Available with varying power outputs, the Eagle range was all based on the same 12.17 litre block and enjoyed a high degree of common parts. Engineering excellence was assured from a company that produced crankshafts which were still within

original tolerances after 20,000 hours and 1,800,000,000 revolutions.
This Guest 400, like so many of the fleet, proudly displays a Rolls-Royce badge on its grille.

(Photo: Marcus Lester)

VGR 808V had a lucky escape when this tipping operation went horribly wrong in August 2001. Remarkably the unit stayed upright and only suffered one broken spring, despite the obvious strain that was put through the chassis. Had it been flipped, the then 21-year-old unit would almost certainly have been written off.
Note the cylindrical aluminium diesel tank, taken from a scrap 401, which Les fitted in 2000 after the original steel tank began to leak, and the 4-11 numerals on the grille strip. *(Photo: Les Baston)*

In 2002 Les fitted VGR 808V with a vertical exhaust stack. This replaced the original 400 system, which ran parallel to the chassis and finished with the silencer right by the nearside rear wheels. Silencer life was understandably poor and Les found it necessary to weld in a new back plate every two years. The second-hand item came from a Foden in a scrap yard and cost £50. After ten years' service on the 400, and its previous existence, it was still in very good condition and Les had recouped the outlay many times over. A trailer full of empty potato boxes makes an impressive load in this 2009 photograph. *(Photo: Les Baston)*

Still hard at it in 2012, VGR 808V looks stunning as it basks in the sunshine with this load of steel fabrications for a farm shed.

After 19 years of faithful service, the original E290 Cummins was about ready for new pistons and liners. However, the offer of an intercooled E320 taken from a Munro Transport Leyland Roadtrain was too good an opportunity to pass up. The Roadtrain's rear-mounted turbocharger suited the 400's narrow chassis well and made the whole installation possible. With the intercooler placing more demand on the cooling system, Les also decided to ditch the unreliable Dynair fan in favour of a viscous type from an L10 Cummins. The new engine gave the old truck a useful boost in power and the potential of another 20 years or so of service. Although it is much developed from the original truck that left the Oldham factory way back in 1980, VGR 808V is a remarkable testament to the 400's longevity. However, without Les and his extraordinary devotion and care this particular truck's story would undoubtedly have ended many years ago. *(Photo: Les Baston)*

66

The building material supply industry was largely responsible for the development and adoption of vehicle-mounted cranes in the late 1970s. The recession-hit building sector contracted in the mid-1970s and, combined with changes in employment tax and increased liability insurance, saw on-site manpower shrink dramatically. Getting unloaded in these circumstances became increasingly difficult and with driver's hours now limited by the tachograph, a solution had to be found. The on-board crane was the obvious answer, especially with loads that could be readily handled in blocks, such as bricks. Even the weight penalty of such a device was easily countered by the increased productivity. This smart example with centre-mounted crane is typical of the breed. Note the steel wings for the second steering axle, a feature of the 30-ton, 8x4 haulage chassis, which was otherwise much the same as the tipper version. *(Photo: Seddon Atkinson Historic Archive)*

With the last 400s being registered in the 1980/81 model years, there were plenty with enough life left in them to operate at the new 38-tonne limit following its introduction in 1983. Trucks fitted with the Rolls-Royce 290, 320 or Cummins E290 would have been ideally suited to such operation and with the big sleeper cab providing plenty of space, TIR work was a very real possibility. Most operators tackling continental runs with a 400, such as this fine example, would opt for Cummins power for its serviceability beyond UK shores where the Rolls-Royce units were virtually unknown. Note the catwalk, additional 40-gallon tank and the unusual – for a Seddon Atkinson – half rear wings.

(Photo: David Wakefield)

Although a 30-ton haulage/tipper chassis, the original Gardner 6LXB fitted to this 400 was found wanting by this Wiltshire operator at this weight. Due to the proximity of the bodywork, the longer 8LXB would not fit, so a Cummins 220 was installed. The factory had not offered the Cummins 220 in this chassis for some time, having offered the 250 instead. However, even though the fuel consumption suffered, the extra 20, or so, bhp seemed to solve the issue for Martins Transport. Note the drop side bodywork, which allowed this truck to handle solid loads like loose sand and aggregates or the concrete slabs seen here. *(Photo: Adrian Cypher)*

Despite its suitability, the 400 was not as prolific as some types in the role of a wrecker. As the sleeper cab was not available from the factory on any multi-wheel rigid chassis, it is reasonable to assume that this smart 400 wrecker was actually based on a stretched tractor chassis. Alternatively, given that it appears to be sitting rather high, the cab may have been grafted onto the chassis of something completely different. Whatever the truck's origin, it made an impressive sight, particularly with this most unusual load behind it. *(Photo: Adrian Cypher)*

Wilkinson Transport continued to purchase 400 series tractor units from S A Trucks, Bristol in 4x2 guise at a rate of up to 20 a month. Buying switched to the 401 when it replaced the 400 and by 1982 Wilkinson operated around 100 examples of the two types, which represented about half of the fleet at the time. Here the latest batch of 400s, on W-registrations from 1980/81, is seen at Wilkinson's then new maintenance facility at Nuneaton. Henry Dilloway continued to supply Wilkinson through the company's changes to Lex Wilkinson and later Federal Express after the US giant purchased the business in 1985. Note the wider roof spoilers fitted to these examples compared to the earlier one on page 31.

(Photos: Courtesy of Henry Dilloway)

The combination of box van trailers and an intensive trunking operation, which saw the majority of the fleet racking around 110,000 miles a year, mainly on motorways and laden 98 percent of the time, meant that even the smallest increase in mpg per unit could yield huge savings on diesel costs for a fleet the size of Wilkinson. As well as being early pioneers of roof spoilers, the company also experimented with speed controllers and found that an E290-powered 400 or 401 fitted with both could achieve up to 9 mpg. This was an improvement of 1.4 mpg over a unit equipped with neither device.

Although, as here, day cabs made up the majority of the fleet, a few 400 and 401 units with sleeper cabs were also on the strength.

(Photo: Courtesy of Henry Dilloway)

Cadbury, despite being by far the smaller of the two companies, got top billing following its merger with Schweppes in 1969 and Cadbury management took a leading role in the running of the new company.

These late 400s were among the last in a long line operated by Cadbury Schweppes, which stretched back to early P-registered examples. Payload was important on the company's own-account work and ultra-light Bedford TM3800s joined the fleet in 1978/79. However, despite the improved payload, the GM machines did not oust the Oldham product, as evidenced here by these W-registered units.

Note the chequer plate modification on the front wings, which was commonly applied to the company's 400s. *(Photo: Marcus Lester)*

This 400 with 401 grille has more right to the upgrade than most as it was registered post-August 1981 after the first 401s had started to appear on W-registrations some months earlier. There was originally a suggestion that the two models would be sold alongside each other, but this seems unlikely and the shifting of old stock, or pre-registration, seems a more likely reason for such late-registered examples of the 400. Although wearing Oakley's normal colours, the striped livery of this example would appear to have been influenced by that of the factory demonstrators doing the rounds for Seddon Atkinson's dealers at the time. *(Photo: Adrian Cypher)*

UMS 458X was another very late example registered post-August 1981. The unit, fleet name 'Grange Earl', was the last of six Gardner-powered 400s operated by John Mitchell. The truck, originally a day cab, featured a Jennings sleeper conversion, as is evidenced by the rearmost window, which is not recessed, and the horizontal bottom profile of the panel in which it is mounted. The curtainsider trailer, a Boalloy Tautliner, was one of the first in the company's trailer fleet, which until then had comprised flats and skeletals for containers. *(Photo: John W Henderson)*

The UK 8x4 tipper market typically generated sales of around 3,000 chassis a year when times were good. Leyland was the class leader in the early 1980s with around 35 percent of the market. The company's Scammell-branded Routeman had ruled the roost for many years and its replacement, the Constructor 8, looked set to do the same. Seddon Atkinson's market share was somewhat less than Leyland's and with priority for the new 401 placed on tractor units, the 8x4 400 was to soldier on until 1983, resulting in some late registrations such as this Y-plate example. The Motor Panels cab still looked fresh in 1983 and, with suitable modifications, was poised for another five years of service on the 401 and 4-11. Although some way short of the amazing 24 years of service that Berliet/Renault extracted from its KB2400 cab, it was on a par with other long-serving designs such as DAF's F241, as used on the 2800. *(Photo: Marcus Lester)*

The 401
S A goes one better

Seddon Atkinson was taken over by the US giant International Harvester (IH) before the launch of the 400 range in 1975. Original approaches had been made as early as 1971, but it was not until the summer of 1974 that the American company actually bought out the shares and took control. By that time the 400 was virtually ready for production and launch, which meant that IH had no input in the design of the new truck, a situation which would be drastically different with its 1981 replacement – the 401.

The 400, always a strong seller from day one, had been subject to constant development and improvement during its first five years of production and by 1980 represented a strong presence in the top-weight sector of the UK. However, the industry had been on the ropes for much of that time and the pressure on manufacturers for more efficient trucks was constant. The 400, along with other trucks using proprietary engines, had moved on strides in terms of better mpg figures with the introduction of Cummins' E-series engines in 1978. With that aspect addressed, the next area for improvement was payload, which meant putting the 400 on a diet!

American truck manufacturers have a long tradition of producing premium trucks that, by European standards, have remarkably low tare weights. For example, a 300 bhp plus 6x4 tractor with a full sleeper cab weighing in at 7 tons would not be unusual. Extensive use of aluminium, particularly in cabs, wheels and tanks had much to do with this. With this approach in mind, work was started on a light-weight version of the 400 with much of the development and testing being carried out in IH facilities in the USA.

The starting point was the chassis, which now incorporated new cross members taken directly from IH's S-class truck in the States. These were a back-to-back, pressed steel design, which, as well as reducing weight, were actually stronger than the fabricated steel items fitted to the 400. The minimum leaf, parabolic suspension was revised with new hanger brackets; anti-roll bars were again deemed unnecessary and the spring leaves were un-shackled. The old steel diesel tank was replaced by an 80-gallon, cylindrical item made of aluminium, which was now, generally, to be mounted on the offside of the chassis. The four-segment spigot mounting system of the wheel hubs allowed aluminium alloy road wheels to be offered as an option and while the alloy wheels were expensive – costing £900 in 1981 – they did offer the potential for massive weight savings over conventional steel items. They also thoroughly enhanced the appearance of the truck if fitted.

At the front of the chassis was a new bumper. Steel-backed, the new one-piece item was made of SMC (sheet moulding compound) and was usually fitted with a stylish and aerodynamic bolt-on, under-bumper air dam. The whole assembly was mounted slightly higher than that of the 400 and housed new quartz halogen headlights, which answered the criticism levelled at the dip-beam performance of the 400. Above and behind the bumper was a new aluminium radiator, which now incorporated its own header tank and filler. The new radiator not only saved weight, it offered improved durability and also negated the need for the old expansion tank/filler arrangement of the 400, which was messily mounted on the rear cab support and required protracted plumbing through to the radiator with the obvious potential for leaks. Perhaps because of the new radiator installation and its aluminium construction, the extra bank of warning lights now fitted in the dashboard included a water temperature light in addition to the water temperature gauge.

Slightly larger S-cam brakes, a lighter ZF steering box and the standard fitment of the group RA-57 single reduction axle completed the chassis.

Perhaps the most striking feature of the 401 was the re-worked Motor Panels cab, which received extensive attention both inside and out creating a good-looking truck with strong driver appeal. Further use of SMC was made for the new grille – which saw the return of the big 'A' logo, front panels and both parts of the front wings. This not only saved weight over steel, it also meant that these high-risk panels were more resistant to knocks and damage and no longer susceptible to corrosion. To further inhibit rust, the doors – now featuring flush-fit handles from the IH parts bin – and the cab floor pressings were coated with Zintec prior to painting. Indeed, the whole cab structure now underwent a seven-stage paint process – such was the desire of Seddon Atkinson to address the rust issue of the 400.

The two new steps, of a stout aluminium design, made cab access a simple affair and, with great attention to detail, these were now lit from above for entry at night. Once inside, the driver was greeted by an expanse of warm brown carpet across the floor and engine tunnel, which was complemented by seats finished in beige velour with an attractive herringbone pattern. The beige velour extended to the cab sides and headlining, the latter a distinct and cosier improvement over the 400's perforated plastic offering. The rather basic Cox seating of the 400 was replaced in the 401 with Bostrum's far superior 303 type, which for the driver included an integral suspension system fully adjustable to weight. The Bostrum seats won immediate praise from road testers of early 401s who found them easily adjustable, comfortable and supportive. The double bunk option was no longer offered for the 401; instead the single bunk was raised to a height just below that of the side windows to provide a cavernous 12 cu ft storage space below. This, combined with pockets in the header rail and rear window apertures, answered another criticism of the 400 and provided the driver with ample space to stow belongings; there was even a fitted suitcase. New roller sun blinds that ran on a metal loop in the centre of the windscreen – much like Ford's Transcontinental and Leyland's T45 Roadtrain – were fitted to accommodate the needs of drivers of less-than-average height and the whole cab could be shut off at night with thick, warm curtains.

The instrument panel, though essentially the same as that of the 400, was revised, as mentioned, with extra warning lights. The dashboard had a new raised centre section, complete with big 'A' and 401 logo, which now housed new sliding controls and vents for the powerful twin, two-speed heaters. The lockable glove-box lid was also raised to the same height and angle to present a smart and ergonomic dashboard. Running down from the centre section of the dash to the engine tunnel was the new drop-down fuse box which contained all the circuit breakers and fuses for the truck's 24-volt electrics. The system also incorporated an earth-leakage detector to warn of a wiring fault.

To resolve one of the 400's worse points, Seddon Atkinson's engineers drastically changed the gear linkage arrangements for the 401. The new lever, itself a more comfortable user-friendly design, was now mounted on top of the engine in the same manner as most other manufacturers. This did away with the troublesome extra linkage that was required with the remote lever installation of the 400. Not only did this make gear changes slicker, it also reversed the gate to the more conventional pattern that climbed up the box as the lever was moved towards the driver. The new lever utilised a rubber boot with a bellows design to seal against the cab floor when lowered and was incorporated in a smart new housing on the engine tunnel that also contained the revised parking-brake lever, which now had an easier forward/aft action.

At the back of the cab, an area already cleaned up by the removal of the 400's header tank, was a new cab-mounting bracket that incorporated a self-locking mechanism that engaged automatically as the cab was lowered onto it. Another new warning light on the dashboard warned the driver if the cab release was unlocked. Also at the back of the cab was a new and purposeful looking air stack, which reached over the top of the roof to catch fresh air for the turbocharger. The latter, incidentally, would now be installed more ergonomically alongside the engine in all installations, rather than at the rear as had been the case with the 400 series. For trucks with Cummins and Gardner engines, the air stack ran up the right-hand rear of the cab, while on Rolls-Royce-engined examples it was mounted on the left.

The 401 was announced, if not launched, at the NEC show in 1980. However, industrial action at IH plants in the US coupled with the worsening market situation in the UK, which ultimately resulted in Seddon Atkinson shutting down its heavy truck facility at Walton-le-Dale with the loss of 800 jobs, conspired to hold up production. Originally sold alongside the 400, customer deliveries of 401s started in 1981 and by the autumn registrations of the new model were growing appreciably.

Despite the broadly similar appearance and obvious ancestry, the 401 was far more than just a light-weight development of the 400. It was a better truck in every respect, particularly driver comfort. With its strong performance, improved serviceability and greater payloads thrown into the mix it ticked the box for drivers, fitters, managers and accountants, something that only a very few trucks have ever pulled off.

MVM 287W was an early factory demonstrator and one of 70 pre-production vehicles completed at Oldham before the end of 1980. Despite the events that threatened to hold up production, advance orders for the 401 ran to £2.5 m.

MVM 287W had completed extensive trials with an oil company and was, unusually, fitted with an anti-lock braking system. *Commercial Motor* put it through its paces on its Scottish test route, where the Cummins E290, which gave 275 bhp at 1,900 rpm and 912 lb-ft of torque at 1,300 rpm, returned just under 7 mpg at an average speed of 41.01 mph. Not bad for the first truck to run the test with the magazine's new box van trailer.

Pictured much later in life and running at 38 tonnes, the unit carries the 'dazzle' livery of John Marsh and Blackpool Van Transport. Since its early days as a demonstrator, the unit has been fitted with a large roof spoiler and the diesel tank has been moved to the nearside. The original double side window has also been changed to this single item and the rear window blanks removed, all presumably for improved visibility.

(Photo: Adrian Cypher)

This handsome unit was another early factory demonstrator that started doing the rounds in 1981. The unit often hauled this matching hospitality trailer to truck and county shows around the UK, often in support of the local dealerships, such as here for S A Commercials, Bristol at this very wet, Royal Bath & West Show (Top). On occasions it was also in the company of a 400 demonstrator, complete with a test-weight loaded trailer, which bore the close registration MVM 283W. Note the legend in the headboard, perhaps a strap line that was never applied to the 401 advertising campaign? *(Photos: Adrian Cypher & Henry Dilloway)*

The W-registration of this 401 marks it out as an early example of the breed. The factory demonstrator livery, trade plate in the windscreen and test-weight load all suggest that the unit may well have been under some trial by Seddon Atkinson, one of its suppliers or a magazine. Given that the truck is pulling a tri-axle trailer suitable for 38-tonne operation, it could have been under evaluation for the weight increase under the Armitage Report of 1983. If so, the unit would have been a couple of years old by that time and possibly kept by the factory for test and development work.

[Photo: Seddon Atkinson Historic Archive]

Through the 1970s the Elddis fleet was virtually an all-Volvo affair. The F88 impressed greatly and led to its replacement, the F10, becoming the tractor of choice towards the end of the decade. However, when economics dictated that the fleet's tractors would have to serve five rather than two to three years, problems started to emerge and, as the company did not consider the fuel consumption to be great either, other makes started to get a look-in at the company's Consett base. This early 401 was one of a number of Seddon Atkinsons that joined the fleet in the early 1980s, along with trucks from ERF, DAF, Leyland, Mercedes and Scania.

The Cummins E290, as fitted here, recorded a 2 mpg improvement over the Volvo F10s. However, when the company's remaining Volvos started to operate at 38 tonnes, they continued to return the same mpg as they had at 32 ton.

Note the Leggett 400 in the background. *(Photo: Marcus Lester)*

Prestons of Potto, being staunch 400 users, were also among the select few that operated early W-registered 401s. This example, NDC 82W, looks particularly good in the company's red-and-white livery with this smart van trailer in tow. Prestons did not put an age limit on its trucks and found that Cummins-powered 400 and 401 units gave three useful lives with an engine rebuild every million miles or so. Even once retired, old units would be retained rather than sold to provide useable spares for the working fleet. *(Photo: Seddon Atkinson Historic Archive)*

Despite the excellent reception afforded to the 401 and the company's high hopes for the future, all was not well at Seddon Atkinson in 1981. Production was down by nearly 40 percent while the company tried to reduce stock of components and finished trucks at a time when the UK heavy truck market had dropped by over a thousand chassis a month. With depressed sales in the US, the parent company was suffering, too, and unfortunately, the axe had to fall somewhere. Identified in a cost-cutting exercise, the victim was to be the Walton-le-Dale assembly plant, which closed with the loss of some 800 jobs.

This was one of a number of early 401 units that were operated alongside 400s by the Mordav Coal Company Ltd. *(Photo: Marcus Lester)*

Now sadly gone, the demise of Beresford must be linked to the collapse of UK's manufacturing industry and the cut-throat rates of large haulage concerns. In happier times, Beresford started to purchase 401 units following good service from previous 400s. For many years, the strong loyalty to domestic products saw the fleet mainly comprising trucks from ERF, Seddon Atkinson and Foden. Foreign infiltration, when it eventually became inevitable, came in the form of DAF, MAN and Volvo. Although Beresford's Seddon Atkinsons were generally powered by Rolls-Royce engines, this example has an air stack mounted on the wrong side for that type of engine; therefore it must be either Cummins or Gardner powered.

(Photo: Marcus Lester)

The 401 interior offered a refined and luxurious environment for the driver that was the match of any continental machine at the time. The carpeted floor and engine tunnel combined with attractive seat and bunk materials in warm shades to give a cosy, yet fresh feel to the interior. Storage was greatly improved by the raised bunk position, which created a large 12 cu ft locker underneath, and by the change to roller blinds, which allowed a decent header rail to be installed above the windscreen. The header rail not only contained a built-in clock and radio position, but also provided handy storage pockets for the driver and passenger, the openings of which were covered by elasticated material to stop items dropping out.

The central loop and side guides for the blinds were revised in 1983 and extended down to the dashboard. *(Photo: Author's collection)*

This nicely presented 401 was working at 38 tonnes post-1983 and it is reasonable to assume it was Cummins powered – such was the popularity of the big 14-litre engines at the time. However, Gardner installations used the same offside location for the air stack, and, as 401s had no designation badges, it's just possible that an example of the latter was under the cab.

When Seddon Atkinson launched the 401 in 1981 it listed two Gardner engine options: the 6LXC and the 8LXC. The 6LXC was the latest development of the famous straight-six design. A normally aspirated unit, it produced 193 bhp and 567 lb-ft of torque from its 10.45 litres, just enough for 32-ton work. The 8LXC, the other choice for Gardner fanciers, was normally aspirated and like the 6LXC, it was the latest version of the type and now developed 257.6 bhp and 740 lb-ft of torque. A 4x2 401 fitted with the 8LXC had a design GCW of 40,000 kg and, although power was marginal, it could have been put to work at 38 tonnes. *(Photo: David Wakefield)*

The 400 series was by no means perfect. Among its problems were the strange gear pattern with a complicated linkage, an electrical box that was vulnerable to water ingress and cabs that could rot badly. However, a very good number of 400 operators stayed with Seddon Atkinson when it introduced the 401 in 1981, so experiences were not all bad. The 400 was rugged, reliable and easy to service and repair. The factory was supportive and proactive, actively seeking feedback all the time and improving the product accordingly.

John Raymond Transport of Bridgend, Wales was one such operator. Swayed by the 400's good points and following excellent service from S A Trucks in Bristol, the company was ordering 401 units as soon as the model was available from the factory. This early example, freshly delivered, is awaiting the finishing touches to the smart red-and-white John Raymond livery. *(Photo: Marcus Lester)*

There can be a little hesitancy from operators regarding new truck models, especially those, like Beecham Vitamealo, which were enjoying reliable service from the existing product. Seddon Atkinson and IH had a great deal invested in the 401 and were not going to send it into the fray without serious back-up. In addition to the 47 distributors that were in place throughout the UK at the time of the 401's launch, a state-of-the-art distribution centre was opened near Preston. Costing a whopping £2.5 m, the new centre was over twice the size of the previous facility and housed 30,000 lines with a stock value of £5.5 m. With another £5 m worth of spares situated throughout the distributorships, this was enough to allay the fears of the most sceptical operators. *(Photo: Marcus Lester)*

In the good old days before accountants ran haulage companies to the bottom line and vinyl wraps had yet to be invented, Eddie Stobart Ltd, like every other operator that wanted its own livery, had its trucks sprayed and sign-written in the time-honoured way. The results had a depth of colour that was arguably more pleasing than the modern method, as is seen here with this smart Cummins-powered 401.

BTR Permali of Gloucester manufactured the smart new grille of the 401 for Seddon Atkinson from a strong and hardwearing thermosetting plastic, a material commonly known as SMC (sheet moulding compound).

Note the driver has affixed a Silver Knight badge to the grille, possibly suggesting experience with older Atkinsons? *(Photo: Seddon Atkinson Historic Archive)*

Even without the company name being present, it would be hard to have mistaken these smart 401s as belonging to any fleet other than John Raymond. The Welsh operator's appetite for day cabs continued unabated with the 401. The attractive unladen weight was probably a key factor for those of its tractors engaged on accounts such as this for Rockwool. All of the company's early 401s were powered by the Cummins E290 and were geared for motorway work with the Fuller nine-speed gearbox and low ratio back axle.
Note the wind-down spare wheel carrier fitted to LWN 841X and the 400 day cab parked beside it, which was also on contract to Rockwool. *(Photo: Marcus Lester)*

Although it is mostly out of shot in this photograph, the older John Raymond 400 makes an interesting comparison with the two new 401s. One of the key areas of improvement on the new models was the cab, particularly the interior. Raising the bunk position and changing the profile of the outer panel above the front wings, as can be seen here, created a generous storage space inside. The change was for the best, but it did mean the end of the optional exterior lockers, which were good for storing items that drivers did not want in the cab, such as wet ropes, oil cans and tools. Also visible is the new profile of the two-piece front wings, which were now made of durable SMC rather than the rust-prone steel used on the 400. *(Photo: Marcus Lester)*

Goldwell were part of the mighty Allied-Lyons Company and fell within its Showerings drinks group. Although it operated autonomously, Goldwell's fleet purchasing policy was steered from Head Office in Shepton Mallet, which enjoyed a close working relationship with S A Trucks of Bristol, suppliers of all the group's vehicles.

However, Goldwell did have some specific requirements for the distribution of its products, Snowball and Country Manor Perry. Some time earlier, the company had switched from artics to drawbars to improve flexibility and ease congestion in its small premises in Kent. As there was no drawbar option for the 401, it was necessary to perform a chassis stretch on a tractor unit. S A Trucks probably carried out the work, though Tachograph Services, also owned by Showerings, were also capable of such an adaptation and later converted 201 rigids into drop-frame distribution trucks. Although replacing well-regarded DAFs, the 401 was well received and prompted two further orders from Goldwell. FYB 441Y and FYB 443Y were purchased in 1983 and although mechanically identical to this example, with Rolls-Royce 265L engines and nine-speed Fuller boxes, they were fitted with curtainsider bodies.

Note the 401 and hospitality trailer behind.

(Photos: Marcus Lester)

From its very inception the 400, and therefore the 401, had been designed for petrol tanker operations. Key to this was the cab design, which deliberately did not feature a rear quarter-light window of the type found on Scania's modular design. While this may have been desirable for over-the-shoulder vision, their inclusion would have made it hard for the cab to conform to pet regs.

The type proved very popular with the oil companies: Shell, Esso and BP ordered some 300 examples between them in the late 1970s. Seddon Atkinson 401s, such as this, followed from 1981. In 1985, BP placed Seddon Atkinson's biggest single order for some time when, as part of a fleet replacement scheme, it ordered another 67 trucks.

(Photo: Marcus Lester)

Air Products started producing gases for industry in the UK in the late 1950s. An early preference for AEC trucks, including Mandators and Mammoth Minors with Ergomatic cabs in the 1960s, gave way to Seddon Atkinson products in the 1970s. The company ran large numbers of 400s, with 401s being added to the fleet as soon as they became available. Being a 'blue chip' company with an interesting product and operation, Air Products' trucks would often crop up in Seddon Atkinson brochures and literature.

The company manufactured the distinctive trailers at its dedicated Acrefair works. *(Photo: Marcus Lester)*

Wilkinson Transport's Chief Engineer, Allan Scandrett, takes the wheel of the company's first 401 tractor in November 1981. The truck was the 100th Seddon Atkinson in the Wilkinson fleet and was handed over by Bob Johnson, then MD of Seddon Atkinson, while S A Commercials' Sales Manager, Henry Dilloway, looked on. Wilkinson Transport was an important customer for S A Commercials of Bristol and Henry managed all the sales into its fleet. Also present at this important handover was Wilkinson's MD, Colin Millbanks, and Seddon Atkinson's Retail Sales Manager, Peter Whitaker. *(Photo: Seddon Atkinson Historic Archive)*

This rear three-quarter view of an MOD 401 of the Royal Navy clearly shows the 400 series diesel tank in situ. The old type offered the same 80-gallon capacity as the new cylindrical version. The steel construction was significantly heavier, but more durable and easier to fix in the field.

This view also shows how the air stack arrangement of the day cab tractor went through a hole in the drop wing. If a sleeper cab were fitted, then the air stack would descend beside the drop wing and then be piped back up through the same hole.

Note the sturdy towing eye and pin installed on the rear cross member on MOD versions. *(Photo: Seddon Atkinson Historic Archive)*

The UK's much anticipated weight limit increase came into effect on 1 May 1983. The new maximum of 38 tonnes was only permitted on a five-axle combination, meaning either the unit or the trailer would require three axles. Most truck manufacturers were quick to offer a 6x2 layout of some description; some even had existing designs that were already in production. However, it soon became clear that operators opting for three axles on the unit, rather than the trailer, favoured a twin-steer layout. Seddon Atkinson announced its twin steer in July 1983. The Oldham solution was actually a two-pronged approach whereby the 301 and 401 twin-steer chassis were launched simultaneously. Both were intended to take on 38-tonne operation. The super light 301, powered by the Cummins LT10, was aimed at the cost- and payload-conscious entry-level operator, while the 401, with Cummins or Rolls-Royce engines of around 300 bhp, was designed for those on prestige, long-haul work. This early example was part of an operation set up in the UK by the DFDS shipping line. *(Photo: Adrian Cypher)*

Dudley Yates of Yates Transport started the first self-drive hire company in Maidstone. Dudley would purchase Transit vans six at a time from Ian Walker, the sales manager at Haynes of Maidstone. Ian also sold him one of the bigger A-series chassis, fitted with a drop-side body. Dudley later passed this vehicle to his son, Neil, who converted it into a wrecker and started his own recovery business, NYR (Neil Yates Recovery). Neil's Kent-based fleet is now one of the largest in the UK and features some stunning machinery.
(Photo: David Wakefield)

Louis Rothman founded his tobacco company in 1890 and soon enjoyed premises on Pall Mall and a Royal Warrant from King Edward VII – such was the quality of his products. In the 1970s and '80s the company became prolific in the sponsorship of motorsports and, rather bizarrely, athletics. The giant British American Tobacco bought the company and its portfolio in 1998. Whether this 1983 example actually hauled cigarettes at some time or was liveried up in association with some sponsorship deal is unknown, but it certainly bears an appropriate registration plate! *(Photo: David Wakefield)*

Seddon Atkinson didn't introduce the 401 8x4 tipper/haulage chassis until 1983, production until then having been concentrated on the tractor versions of the new model. In the interim, the 400 had soldiered on in this traditional role, but a strong pound and competent foreign alternatives had slashed its market share dramatically by 1982. SMW 648Y, chassis no. 75450, was the first 401 tipper chassis produced. It rolled off the production line in January 1983. The truck was bought new by Blackford's Landscaping Services of Greenhill near Swindon, where it replaced a three-year-old 400.

The spec included twin lifting rams by Edbro and, although curiously shut in this photograph, the capacious Wilcox body was fitted with side-hinged doors rather than a tailgate.

(Photo: Seddon Atkinson Historic Archive)

This handsome 401, built in July 1982, was fitted with the Rolls-Royce 290L, the middle of three engines from that manufacturer offered by Seddon Atkinson for the 401 at the time of launch. Like Cummins, Rolls-Royce offered different outputs from essentially one engine, in this case a 12.17-litre straight six known as the Eagle. The entry-level 265L produced 256 bhp and 792 lb-ft of torque while the 290L produced 281 bhp and 868 lb-ft of torque. At the top of the range was the 320, which didn't carry the L suffix. Originally, this was the most powerful engine in terms of bhp available in the 401; it produced 311 bhp and 870 lb-ft of torque. Note the lovely wide axle spread tilt behind this example and the Volvo F86 in the far background.

[Photo: Seddon Atkinson Historic Archive]

Blackford's were used to running the normally aspirated Gardner 6LXC in its 400 series tippers and rated the unit for its economy and reliability, but the extra power of the turbocharged 6LXCT – now the standard Gardner option for the tipper chassis – significantly improved on-road performance. The weight saving of the Gardner unit, which made use of aluminium alloys in its design, over the alternative Rolls-Royce 265L, the other standard engine for this chassis, allowed Blackford's to realise a payload of just under 20 tonnes.
Note that the operator has found it necessary to brace the bottom step, which was low and vulnerable to damage when off road.
(Photo: Adrian Cypher)

This smart tipper operated by R J Hardy and Son represents the Rolls-Royce-powered alternative in the 8x4 chassis. When installed in the 401, the 265L produced 256 bhp and 792 lb-ft of torque. Although it carried a weight penalty over the Gardner 6LXCT, the greater torque of the Rolls-Royce 265L – some 153 lb-ft greater – stood it in good stead for operators on tougher tipper work. Since the Rolls-Royce produced its peak torque at 200 rpm less than the Gardner, its longevity and potential fuel economy could also be assured.
The driver of this example certainly seems proud to be sitting above a Rolls-Royce engine, stating its presence under the cab with numerous bumper stickers. *(Photo: Marcus Lester)*

Another of Harwich Transports twin-steer 401s, but the factory paint scheme here suggests that this Cummins-powered example was an ex-demonstrator.

Following the introduction of 38-tonne operation in the UK, many companies handling trailers that were collected from ports opted for the twin-steer arrangement. With no control over how a trailer was loaded, the layout guarded against overloading the unit's rear axles.

The distinctive one-piece rear wing makes the distance between the rear axles seem incredibly big. It was, in fact, 4 ft 6 in, which was identical to that of the rival product from DAF. *(Photo: Marcus Lester)*

No doubt the 401's incredibly low fighting weight was a factor in its adoption into the massive Pandoro fleet. The lightest chassis was the T17 G23 equipped with a standard wheelbase of 10 ft 3 in and fitted with a day cab; it tipped the scales at just 5,430 kg (with aluminium wheels). However, the output of the Gardner 6LXCT fitted to that model restricted its GCW to 36.5 tonnes. Operators requiring the lightest possible 401 for 38-tonne work would have to opt for the Rolls-Royce-powered T17 R26 or T17 R30, which came in at 5,560 kg. Pandoro probably specified this example with a Cummins E290, as it did in later 401 twin-steer units, which, despite the engine's large 14-litre capacity, still had a commendable chassis cab weight of 5,680 kg – comfortably under 6 tonnes. *(Photo: Adrian Cypher)*

GAT 351Y, seen here at the head of an impressive line-up of Seddon Atkinson vehicles belonging to Feedex Q-Feeds, was another early example of the new 401 tipper chassis built in March 1983. Twin-leaf parabolic front springs replaced the 400's semi-elliptic, multi-leaf arrangement for the new chassis which brought a great improvement in ride characteristics. Norde rubber suspension was an option for the rear.
This example was fitted with the Rolls-Royce 265L, nine-speed Fuller gearbox and IH RA472 single-reduction axles; the latter two items now being the standard fit for the tipper/haulage chassis.

(Photo: Seddon Atkinson Historic Archive)

Gardner was reticent about following its competitors down the turbocharging route and put it off for many years until environmental pressure to clean up emissions and ever-increasing power demands finally dictated its adoption. The first example, the 6LXCT – 'T' denoting turbo – was introduced in 1981, which was the same year as the 401. The new engine, as installed in the Seddon Atkinson chassis, produced 217 bhp – only 24 bhp more than the normally aspirated 6LXC – but, more significantly, it upped the torque by 73 lb-ft. Gardner followed this in 1983 with the 8LXCT, a turbocharged version of the eight-cylinder engine.

This gave the big engine a really useful output of 287 bhp and 865 lb-ft of torque.

This 401 was fitted with the 8LXCT and the loyal customer was proud to advertise the presence of a Gardner engine under the cab.

(Photo: Seddon Atkinson Historic Archive)

The 400 had been equipped with a 14 in Lipe Rollway clutch, which, although a tough unit usually capable of absorbing much punishment and even misuse, had developed something of a reputation for breaking centre springs in this particular installation. Lipe Rollway made modifications to the unit in an effort to solve the problem, but, as with all the 400's maladies, the matter was properly addressed in the 401 through the fitting of a heavy-duty, twin-plate clutch made by Dana Spicer. Still a 14 in design, it featured angled springs, which lowered pedal effort by 35 percent, and was also self adjusting, which greatly improved service times.

(Photo: Marcus Lester)

Seddon Atkinson did much work on quality control in the years leading up to the 401's launch. In 1978 the company became an approved manufacturer for the Ministry of Defence and gained the rigorous O529 standard, which covered trucks. This meant stringent checks by an MOD inspector on a monthly basis to maintain the approved status, which was renewed every two years. The benefits of this, combined with other measures, spilled over to benefit civilian customers, with Oldham producing its best quality trucks yet. Every month, in addition to the usual checks, at least one vehicle was pulled from the line for a thorough examination, which culminated in a 30-mile test drive.

(Photo: Marcus Lester)

Cummins announced changes to its engine-reconditioning scheme in 1983. The main NH, NHC, NT and NTE were all covered with extremely competitive pricing that made a long block replacement through Cummins ReCon the same price as a short block reconditioned engine from many other manufacturers. Cummins also relaxed the minimum requirement for the number of sound components on an engine before reconditioning it. Topped by a generous 12-month unlimited mileage warranty, this scheme made Cummins a very attractive proposition for 401 customers like Charles Footman. *(Photo: Marcus Lester)*

Seddon Atkinson scored a major victory over rivals ERF and Foden when Gardner chose this 401 for its parts distribution service. The truck, chassis number 76455, was built in November 1983 and was, not surprisingly, fitted with a 6LXCT – the turbocharged version of the 10.45-litre, six-cylinder engine – and operated at 32 ton. No doubt Gardner paid very close attention to its operational performance in this role. Gardner engines were more expensive to buy than those of competitors and the situation was made worse by truck manufacturers loading the chassis price for Gardner installation. However, spare parts for Gardner engines were considerably cheaper and the fact that the engines were highly economical had to be considered. *(Photo: Seddon Atkinson Historic Archive)*

By 1983 International Harvester was in a dire financial position and had to abandon its European ambitions in an attempt to save its core business back home. The Company's share in DAF was put up for sale and the plans for ENASA (Pegaso) to produce IH engines in Spain were dropped. Despite several years of losses, partly due to the large redundancy bill from the 1981 lay-offs, Seddon Atkinson, with the 401 still fresh and order books full, was IH's most valuable overseas asset. Although Seddon Atkinson was put up for sale, it was not to be a bargain basement offer: only serious enquiries were considered.

Despite the uncertainty of the company's ownership, 401 sales continued to grow, especially with loyal customers such as W & J Riding, which added this fine example to its fleet in 1983.

[Photo: Seddon Atkinson Historic Archive]

Showerings, the soft drink manufacturer and distributor, was part of the massive Allied-Lyons group. The parent company had a strong loyalty to the Seddon Atkinson brand with the fleets of its various companies usually comprising Oldham-built machines.

The first production 401 twin-steer chassis went to Showerings in the early summer of 1983. The unit was fitted with the Rolls-Royce 290L, Fuller gearbox and Rockwell R180 rear axle. It also featured a Jost sliding fifth-wheel, which offered over half a metre of adjustment, to aid coupling to the company's large trailer fleet. Although the unit was running as a three-plus-three combination here, it is likely that this situation was just circumstantial because the trailer fleet had to include tri-axle trailers to suit the numerous 4x2 units that were operated. *(Photo: Adrian Cypher)*

Despite running a number of other makes in the fleet, Keedwell continued buying Seddon Atkinsons over the years. Having enjoyed good service from the 400s that it operated, the company added 401s soon after the model's launch. The author has very fond memories of riding with his brother-in-law in Keedwell's X-registered example – a 4x2 fitted with a Cummins E290 – when it was brand new. That unit, along with another 4x2, was later converted with a tag axle to operate at 38 tonnes, but this 1983 unit was a genuine factory twin steer.

(Photo: Marcus Lester)

By 1984 Seddon Atkinson were offering the latest E320 from Cummins for the 401, but early models were offered with the choice of two Cummins engines: the 250 Turbo and the E290. Both were based on the same 14-litre block, though only the larger engine was part of the superb NTE family as introduced in 1978. However, the smaller engine was an admirable performer with 231 bhp and a very credible 789 lb-ft of torque – more than an F10 at the time.

This smart 401, operated by a Blackpool-based sweet manufacturer, was fitted with the bigger of the two engines: the E290. The six-cylinder engine delivered 275 bhp and 912 lb-ft of torque, which gave ample power and good economy. In many respects, the E290 was the perfect engine for those on UK long-distance general haulage.

Note the Cunard skeletal being used here by Daintee as another container load of sweets heads for the docks. *(Photo: Seddon Atkinson Historic Archive)*

The positively steered second axle operated at a maximum outward angle of up to 17 degrees. This was somewhat less than the front axle's 40 degree max, but was enough to allow a turning circle of just over 55 ft. This was 10 ft more than the 401 4x2 unit, despite the latter's more modest steering angle of 35 degrees.

Like the 4x2 day cab, the air stack on the twin-steer chassis did not reach down below the chassis rail, but was instead plumbed through the drop wing to free up valuable space on the chassis rail.

This fine selection of early 401 twin-steer units with E290 engines was new to Pandoro at the end of 1983. *(Photo: Seddon Atkinson Historic Archive)*

The 401 twin steer actually shared its chassis with the 301; with the cabs removed the two were virtually indistinguishable. It is a great testament to Oldham's engineers that they were able to create a chassis that would not only mount both cabs, but also cater for the small LT10 Cummins as well as the 401's usual power units. The complete rationalisation of parts helped to keep chassis prices reasonable. Twin-steer versions were typically in the region of £4,500–£5,000 more than the equivalent 4x2 from either range. Interestingly, although all the dimensions from the back of the chassis to the centre of the front axle were the same for the 401 and 301, the latter had a slightly longer front overhang, resulting in a greater overall length (by 26 mm) for the 'smaller' vehicle. Note the 75-gallon diesel tank, which was a special version developed for the twin-steer chassis. *(Photo: Marcus Lester)*

The superb weight savings of the 401 over the outgoing 400 raised many an eyebrow in the industry following the truck's Motor Show debut in the autumn of 1980. Leyland, with its T45 fresh out of the blocks, was so concerned it started to evaluate the possibility of manufacturing the C40 cab in aluminium with a projected weight saving of 200 kg. Such was its disbelief in Seddon Atkinson's claims for the new model that Leyland was also planning to weigh a 401 as soon as the model was generally available.
This fine line-up of 401s belonging to W & J Riding includes an early example registered on a 1981 W-registration. *(Photo: Marcus Lester)*

Speculation over the future of Seddon Atkinson came to an end in March 1984 when ENASA (of Spain) and International Harvester finally crossed the t's and dotted the i's on their agreement. ENASA, which had a strong relationship with IH, were a logical choice. The company also enjoyed a relationship with DAF, which would ultimately benefit all three companies with the joint development of the Cabtec cab some years later.
The announcement of the deal had an immediate affect on output at Oldham, as customers with 'order options' were now happy to proceed. Freightliner may well have been among those customers with this fine 1984 example. *(Photo: Marcus Lester)*

One of the biggest improvements of the 401 8x4 tipper and haulage chassis when compared to the 400 was the additional ram to transmit steering input to the second axle. This followed the practice of the many European manufacturers, the products of which had made a huge impact on this sector of the market since the mid-1970s. The steering revisions brought a big improvement in manoeuvrability over the 400, shaving some 13 ft from the vehicle's turning circle. Apart from changing the floor carpets for more durable rubber mats and a return to the more basic Cox seats, the luxurious 401 cab was unchanged in this application and, unlike the 400, the sleeper version was offered too. A low-height air stack was fitted to allow for overhanging tipper bodies and, for obvious reasons, the under-bumper air dam was removed.

Note the revised lower step that was changed following operator experience with the original design, which was prone to damage. *(Photo: Seddon Atkinson Historic Archive)*

The Rockwell R180 rear axle was a single reduction type with a 10-ton capacity and the front and intermediate axles were each plated for just under 6 tons. This gave the 401 twin-steer chassis a 22-tonne capacity, so this example, fitted with the Cummins E290, would have been officially designated as a T22 C29. By 1984, the other choices in the range were the T22 C32 and T22 R30, which gave twin-steer customers a power choice from 275 to 308 bhp. The twin-steer chassis was competitively light for its class, but an extra 160 kg could be shaved off the unladen weight if the buyer opted for the expensive aluminium wheels. Both parts of this smart combination appear to be new, representing a tidy investment for Peter D Stirling Ltd.

(Photo: Seddon Atkinson Historic Archive)

Hales Cakes of Clevedon operated a unique haulage system for the distribution of its produce, whereby a fleet of artics, operating at around 26 tons, travelled regular set routes stopping along the way to make lay-by transfers to smaller local delivery trucks.

In the early 1980s the trunking fleet numbered 24 trucks – a mix of 400 and 401 units – and 36 trailers. The trucks were all Gardner powered and averaged around 10 mpg. Day cabs were specified as drivers used digs, often in private houses, on nights out. The distribution fleet was made up of petrol-engined Bedford TKs, each driven by a delivery/salesman.

This fine example is fitted with the 6LXCT. This was Gardner's first engine to utilise a turbocharger and was introduced in 1981 and delivered a healthy 230 bhp. *(Photo: Courtesy of Henry Dilloway)*

With new ownership came a new confidence at Seddon Atkinson, which, with 918 chassis produced, saw a massive 50.5 percent increase in output for the first half of 1984. The UK market was picking up and ENASA pumped a whopping half a million pounds into sales promotion activity. However, Prestons needed no incentive and continued purchasing 401s, and the 4-11 after that, for its operations. An example of the latter completed 14 years on the road for the Potto-based company before taking on shunting duties at a steel works. *(Photo: Marcus Lester)*

From the outset, Seddon Atkinson designed the 401 for higher weights than the 400 and plated the 401, in 4x2 configuration, at 40 tons. This tidy example was well under capacity operating at 32 tons. Edwards of Hull were part of Ideal Standard. The company operated a fleet of around 30 trucks, mostly artics, which were primarily used to deliver the parent company's sanitary products to builders merchants throughout the UK but also undertook general haulage duties. This made for an interesting colour combination of the Edwards trucks and Ideal Standard's blue curtainsiders. Other 401s were operated including earlier examples and day cabs.

Ceva Logistics took over the work in 2010, by which time the Edwards fleet was mainly Volvo. *(Photo: Adrian Cypher)*

With no Gardner option listed for the twin-steer chassis, Bulwark had to abandon its former allegiance to the power plants from Patricroft. In the event, it opted for Cummins over Rolls-Royce and took the higher-powered E320 over the E290. This was not the first change in buying practices for Bulwark as the twin-steer 401s were put to work alongside examples of DAF's equivalent chassis, the FTG2800. This well-worked example was overnighting in Swindon when photographed. Note that the under-bumper air dam has been removed, which has necessitated the replacement of the rather nice aluminium lower step with these more basic items in steel. *(Photo: Adrian Cypher)*

Brown's ran a good number of 401 units in this smart livery. The pattern, though not the colour, was loosely based on the late 400 and early 401 demonstrator livery of the factory. The fleet was made up of a mix of 4x2 and twin-steer chassis to operate at 38 tonnes with tri-axle trailers, the six-axle combinations enjoying the tax break allowed for running an extra axle over the minimum requirement. The trucks were top spec and included the costly, but weight saving, aluminium wheel option. Channel hops were a big part of the operation and the trucks frequently carried liquid freight, generally non-hazardous foodstuff like molasses, in stainless tankers. The company also worked the London markets under the GLC exemption scheme. *(Photo: David Wakefield)*

As delicate and valuable loads go, this Tornado GR3 must have been right up at the top. No 2 MT Squadron moved this example using the modern-day version of the famous and distinctive Queen Mary aircraft trailer. The type was first developed by Tasker for the RAF in 1940 to facilitate the transport of recovered aircraft, numbers of which were at an all-time high due to the intense fighting over England during the Battle of Britain. The trailer's nickname came from its comparatively long length, for the era, and was an obvious reference to the famed Cunard Liner of the same name. The wings and tail are being carried, supported in a jig, on another Queen Mary also pulled by a 401. *(Photo: No 2 MT Squadron)*

British Nuclear Fuels Ltd have been responsible for the running of the UK's world-leading nuclear plants since their inception in the late 1950s. Transport of materials and supplies was inevitable and required a small and specialised fleet. Top of the pile were the trucks used to transport spent fuel rods for reprocessing. In 1981 two MAN 32.400s took over this role from a pair of Scammell Contractors. These were true heavy-haulage machines with 6x4 layout and lead-filled ballast boxes, which brought tractor weight up to 23 tons. Trailers were multi-axled well-types by Crane Fruehauf for Gross Train Weights of 95 tonne. The majority of the weight, some 50 tonnes, came from the special safety flask used to contain the spent fuel rods. Nearly indestructible, the flasks were constructed of 14.5 in steel. To allay the fears of the public, BNFL staged a spectacular demonstration in which it rammed a flask with a fast-moving train. The train was totally wrecked, while the container only suffered superficial damage.

No less impressive, these two 401s, fitted with Cummins E320 engines, fulfilled other essential duties for BNFL.

(Photo: Seddon Atkinson Historic Archive)

Despite the olive drab livery, this 401 of No 2 MT Squadron, fitted with a sleeper cab, roof spoiler and pulling a standard York curtainsided trailer, would have passed as a civilian truck to many a casual observer. However, to aid anonymity and allow the movement of military cargo without attracting undue attention, the MOD also operated what was known as the 'white fleet'. As the name suggests, the fleet's trucks were finished in factory white to blend in with everyday traffic. They may even have gone unnoticed, had it not been for their military registrations!
(Photo: No 2 MT Squadron)

Following Gardner's foray into turbocharging with the 6LXCT, there was much pressure from the market for a turbocharged version of the big eight-cylinder engine. Gardner's reply came in 1983 with the 8LXCT, which produced 287 bhp and 865 lb-ft of torque from its 13.93 litre displacement.
As a dedicated user of Gardner-powered 400 and 401 tractors, Leggett received the first production example, PMU 507Y, and closely monitored its performance for the factory as a running evaluation. The truck was also road tested by the magazines *Commercial Motor* and *Truck*. Performance and economy were obviously favourable as at least a further nine examples joined the Leggett fleet. This one appears to be doing a promotional turn for a Seddon Atkinson dealership at a show.
Leggett were first in line again in 1985 when the company took delivery of the first 401 fitted with the new 6LYT engine. This was a totally new six-cylinder design of 15.5-litres, which took over the top role from the old eight-cylinder engines. *(Photo: Adrian Cypher)*

Seddon Atkinson paid great attention to the requests and needs of drivers and operators when it first conceived the 400 series. The process was the same for the 401 with all criticism and comment on the 400 taken into account in its design. One thing that became apparent was that the need for a second bunk was rare for UK-based trucks – even those venturing onto the continent were usually single-manned. It was decided that the company should offer only one bunk in the 401 so that drivers could have more storage in the cab. This allowed the designers to raise the height of the mattress and install a large locker underneath, complete with fitted suitcase. However, due to the height and flat nature of the engine tunnel, it was possible for a second, lithe person to sleep across the seats when necessary.

This smart T22 C32 twin-steer demonstrator was chassis No. 77577, built in July 1984. *(Photo: Seddon Atkinson Historic Archive)*

The dimensions of a Victor fuselage were beyond the capabilities of the Queen Mary trailers of No 2 MT Squadron, so a civilian, extendable, semi-low loader had to be hired in to accommodate its bulk for this interesting move. The Handley Page Victor was the third element of Great Britain's V-Force, designed to deliver the country's nuclear weapons to its enemies, and entered service in 1958. Although the aircraft could break the sound barrier in a gentle dive, it was found to be unsuitable in its intended role and instead became the backbone of the RAF's tanker refuelling fleet.

(Photos: No 2 MT Squadron)

The 308 bhp and 1,083 lb-ft of torque produced by the Cummins Super E320 fitted to this 6x4 401 seems well on top of the task of hauling this impressive earthmover load. The alternative engine for this chassis in 1984 was the Rolls-Royce 300Li, which developed 288 bhp and 916 lb-ft of torque. The installation of the Rolls-Royce engine would have dictated an air stack location on the nearside.

The 6x4 chassis was a masterpiece of compact engineering with a wheelbase of 3,213 mm (10 ft 6.5 in) contained in an overall length of just 5,915 mm (19 ft 5 in).

Note the replacement bumper and the distinct 'Aussie' feel imparted by the front flaps with big 'A' logos, which are mounted underneath.

(Photo: Adrian Cypher)

Suttons' unmistakeable livery, with partial Union Flag treatment, was applied to a large number of 401s. Suttons were an early customer for the 400 taking delivery of the 51st example off the production line in 1975. That original 400 followed a long association with Atkinson trucks and Suttons immediately fitted it with a big 'A' badge, possibly making it the first company to do so. The big 'A' badge, along with some other modifications, created a grille that looked something like that of the 401 some six years before the model appeared and may possibly have inspired Seddon Atkinson's design. *(Photo: Adrian Cypher)*

This 401 of No 2 MT Squadron is coupled to an example of the unit's sliding bogie trailers, which were extensively used for carrying wheeled and tracked vehicles up to the size of a Scorpion tank. Before loading, the bogie was braked and the locking mechanism released. The unit would then reverse back pushing the trailer bed beyond it. The rear of the trailer would drop to the ground as this happened: the bed creating a ramp. The loading process was not for the faint hearted and the unit up front would sometimes need to be attached to something substantial, such as a tank, to stop it from moving. Once loaded, the unit could be pulled forward, bringing the trailer horizontal and the bogie back to its position where it would be locked back into place. *(Photo: No 2 MT Squadron)*

This smart 401 of Smith Bros of Doncaster was the first production 401 to be fitted with the new Rolls-Royce 340Li engine and was supplied by S A Commercials in Scunthorpe.

The 340Li was introduced in 1985. Turbocharged and intercooled, it was the most powerful engine from Rolls-Royce, or any other manufacturer, that was ever officially offered in the 401. The engine developed 328 bhp at 1,950 rpm and 1,047 lb-ft of torque at a low 1,250 rpm. Although it produced 20 bhp more than the Cummins E320, it could not quite match the torque of 1,083 lb-ft at 1,200 rpm, which gave the Cummins engine a 1 percent advantage in gradeability. The Smith's 401 travelled all over the UK with steel loads, as here, and undertook local work deliveries of coal and iron ore to steel plants.

(Photo: Seddon Atkinson Historic Archive)

...and upward! Engine identification became a little easier on later 401 models as it became more common for manufacturers' badges to be fitted. This smart example bore chassis No. 79213 and was produced in May 1985. It was fitted with the 300Li,

which was one of three Rolls-Royce engines offered in the 401 chassis at the time.

Developing 288 bhp and 916 lb-ft of torque, it filled the gap between the 256 bhp 265Li and the 328 bhp 340Li, which made it an ideal choice for UK work at 38

tonnes. If fitted with the 4.30 to one differential, the truck was capable of 73 mph, which meant relaxed and economical cruising at legal motorway speeds.

(Photo: Seddon Atkinson Historic Archive)

The development and introduction of the 15.5-litre 6LYT engine allowed Seddon Atkinson to offer a Gardner option in the 6x2 twin-steer chassis for the first time in 1985. Rationalisation and a study of buying trends had seen the Cummins E290 dropped from this chassis, leaving the E320 as the only Cummins option, while Rolls-Royce added the 340Li to the 300Li. This meant that with the exception of the 300Li, which produced 288 bhp, all the engines offered for the twin steer were over 300 bhp.

This beautifully presented example from James Moffat's fleet makes a splendid combination. No doubt the driver appreciated the 1,007 lb-ft of torque that the Gardner produced on long hauls to and from Scotland, particularly with a hefty load of paper reels as here. The company moved from Cardenden to Dalgety Bay in the 1990s. *(Photo: Marcus Lester)*

Despite the practical business thinking of his son, Michael, Nicholas Grose's enthusiasm for the haulage industry continued unabated and his desire for trying different combinations of truck and engine saw a return of Gardner power units.

The new Gardner 6LYT was a remarkable piece of engineering that embraced many of the company's traditional ideas within a modern engine with a 15.5 litre capacity. The power output of 305 bhp and 1,007 lb-ft of torque was ideal for 38-tonne operation and a weight saving of around 350 lbs over the equivalent Cummins made it an attractive proposition. Operators with a strong Gardner history were quick to try the new engine.

N J Grose used these tank trailers to deliver china clay to the Iggesund paper works in Cumbria at a rate of ten loads per week. *(Photo: Marcus Lester)*

Seddon Atkinson revealed the Silver Knight at the Scottish Motor Show in 1985. The truck was very much a marketing exercise, which, the factory claimed, was aimed at attracting owner-drivers to the 401. Based on a twin-steer chassis with a Rolls-Royce 340Li engine, the Silver Knight was fitted with a host of extras including: a vertical exhaust system, roof spoiler, aluminium wheels, air horns and night heater. The special two-tone silver paint scheme was applied by an outside concern as the Oldham factory did not have the facility at the time. The options were part of the Silver Knight package, but buyers could pick and choose from the list. The show truck, with every option, carried a hefty premium of nearly £5,000 over a standard 401. The roof spoiler was inspired, if not copied, from the Iveco design that was current at the time and was produced by Longton Coachcraft. *(Photo: Seddon Atkinson Historic Archive)*

Following the factory's Silver Knight exercise, a number of Seddon Atkinson dealers took it upon themselves to create their own interpretations of the project. S A Commercials was one such dealer and created the dramatic White Knight without help from the factory by sourcing the extras direct from the respective manufacturers. The truck was built up on a twin-steer chassis similar to the original show truck, which the dealership already had in stock. Although originally a day cab, the truck was converted, with the correct panels, into a sleeper, the only clue to the conversion being a ridge running over the seam above the front wings. Most of the show truck's options, with the exception of the costly aluminium wheels, were present on the Gardner-powered truck and the overall white finish and one-piece rear wings certainly made it stand out.

White Knight was featured on the cover of the 401 brochure for 1986 and S A Commercials used it as a demonstrator for six months, during which time it clocked over 25,000 miles, before it was sold to a regular customer. *(Photos: Henry Dilloway)*

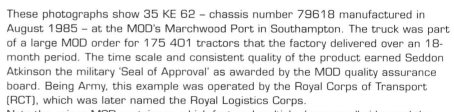

These photographs show 35 KE 62 – chassis number 79618 manufactured in August 1985 – at the MOD's Marchwood Port in Southampton. The truck was part of a large MOD order for 175 401 tractors that the factory delivered over an 18-month period. The time scale and consistent quality of the product earned Seddon Atkinson the military 'Seal of Approval' as awarded by the MOD quality assurance board. Being Army, this example was operated by the Royal Corps of Transport (RCT), which was later named the Royal Logistics Corps.

Note the unique MOD containers, which featured multiple doors on all sides and the logistics landing ship of the Royal Fleet Auxiliary behind. *(Photos: Seddon Atkinson Historic Archive)*

By 1986, truck manufacturers were investing a great deal of time and money into the development of aerodynamic packages for their products. Volvo, Scania and Mercedes were among the class leaders with tailored roof fairings and side screens. Far from tailored, Seddon Atkinson's first attempt was the off-the-peg solution that was offered in the Silver Knight package.

The operator of this fine T17 C32 seems to have fitted something a bit more substantial, which seems well matched to the height of the trailer and is not unlike the raised roof that Seddon Atkinson offered on municipal versions of the 301 and 3-11. *(Photo: Seddon Atkinson Historic Archive)*

If the author is not mistaken, this very late registered 401 was part of Jack Light's fleet based in Holcombe. If so, it speaks highly of the 401 as Jack was not generally a fan of British trucks and certainly did not favour Rolls-Royce engines. Instead he preferred European vehicles – the more powerful the better. Fitted with the big E320 Cummins, power was certainly no problem for this unit; its 308 bhp and 1,086 lb-ft of torque were easily up to the task of 38-tonne operation.

Jack also liked a good bargain; so, as this was among the last 401s, maybe the price was particularly attractive. However, it's just possible, given that he started his business in the 1950s with a Seddon, that a hint of nostalgia crept in too.

Note the latest style of mirrors, which appeared on the last of the 401s. *(Photo: Seddon Atkinson Historic Archive)*

Another late example registered towards the very end of 401 production. The Gardner 270 grille badge means that a 6LXDT engine is lurking under the cab. Introduced in mid-1984, the engine was only available in the 401 for a short period and was not officially offered in the 4-11 chassis. Essentially a bored and stroked version of the 6LXCT, the new engine produced 254 bhp and 827 lb-ft of torque as installed in the 401. The increased torque brought greater flexibility and improved fuel economy, which no doubt endeared it to fuel-conscious operators like W & J Riding which operated this smart example in customer livery. *(Photo: Marcus Lester)*

This well-worked 401 demonstrates why the integral under-bumper air dam was removed from the 8x4 tipper chassis. While attractive and functional on a road truck, its low position and SMC construction made it vulnerable in any rough situation, and this truck clearly operated in plenty of those. This unit was originally a 4x2, but was later fitted with a tag axle. As the Rolls-Royce 290L was only officially being fitted to military chassis by the 1984/85-model year, there is a good chance that it was an ex-MOD example. *(Photo: Adrian Cypher)*

The 4-11
Reaching for the Strato's sphere

In the autumn of 1986 Seddon Atkinson applied an update across all its ranges, which brought the new '-11' suffixes to the model designations. In the case of the 4-11, the changes over the 401, although functional, were mostly cosmetic with mechanical components and layout unchanged.

The most obvious difference was the new one-piece corner deflectors, which now incorporated the indicators. The 400/401 had always suffered from mirror and side window fouling and it was thought that turbulence and muck created by the wheel nuts was largely responsible for this. Trucks fitted with a step ring seemed to fare better and many operators fitted small corner deflectors, too. However, most drivers found the age-old method of attaching a piece of rag, which was free to flap in the airstream, to the mirror arm was generally the best solution. The new corner panel also offered a secure location for a new indicator assembly to replace the Rubbolite item that was prone to damage.

(Photo: Seddon Atkinson Historic Archive)

Shirley's Transport must have been among the first operators to take on the 4-11 with this early example registered somewhere between the model's launch in the autumn of 1986 and the new E-registrations of August the following year. The Seddon Atkinson was something of an interloper amid Shirley's fleet, which was made up almost entirely of Volvo F10s at the time.
Although famed for its smart fleet of stainless steel tankers, the 4-11 is seen here with one of the company's curtainsiders: a type that was also run in numbers alongside bulk tipping trailers. Shirley's Transport have always stuck to a one driver/one truck system where possible and the vehicles are always immaculately turned out as a result. *(Photo: Marcus Lester)*

When the 4-11 was launched in the autumn of 1986 Seddon Atkinson offered the new truck with the Cummins Super E400, which became the most powerful engine that the company ever offered for any 400 series derivative. The engine produced a whopping 388 bhp and a truly prodigious 1,200 lb-ft of torque at 1,300 rpm. The E400 was well suited to heavier applications, but

was maybe a little too much for most prospective 4-11 customers on general haulage. As such, it was deleted as an option on 4x2 and 6x2 chassis in May 1987 and with only limited numbers of 6x4 chassis being sold, it was also dropped from the double-drive chassis by the end of the year.

BOC was a good blue-chip customer for the Seddon

Atkinson, but with no requirement for the output of the E400, it opted for the Super E320 to power this impressive example. The company's highly specialised business necessitated an in-house design and engineering department to build trailers like this amazing oxygen transporter.

(Photo: Seddon Atkinson Historic Archive)

Owens Road Services is a family-owned concern which has managed to thrive and survive in the face of stiff competition from the big corporation style of haulage that has seen many smaller firms either swallowed up or put out of business.

Determination, good management and a strong understanding of customer service has seen the company progress from a one-van outfit in 1970 to a 200 truck operation with multiple depots and warehousing facilities by 2012.

When this late-registered 4-11 was new, the fleet was growing at a steady rate through contracts with the automotive industry and was around 30 vehicles strong – a good medium size for a family-run firm at the time.

(Photo: Adrian Cypher)

Inevitably, R T Keedwell's positive experience with the 400 and 401 led to the purchase of this early 4-11 twin steer soon after the model's introduction. The Super E320-powered 4-11 also gave good service and acted as the stepping stone to Strato ownership for the Somerset haulier.

D750 RYB is pictured with one of the company's early curtainsiders at a time when roped and sheeted flats were still the most common type on the trailer fleet. Note that the 'A' logos on the hub centres have been picked out to highlight them. *(Photo: Adrian Cypher)*

J R Holland & Son started trading in the early 1980s, becoming the J R Holland Group as more aspects were added to the core business of fresh produce. R & N Transport was one such business that fell under the group's umbrella; the company was responsible for the delivery of produce to supermarkets and cash-and-carry warehouses.

The attractively finished T22 C32 4-11 was new in 1987 and was based at R & N Transport's depot on the Portobello Industrial Estate in Birtley, a location that gave the company easy access to the A1. *(Photo: Seddon Atkinson Historic Archive)*

Although these T17 C32 4-11s, of Piggins and Rix, were not quite consecutively registered, they actually came off the production line one after the other. Chassis numbers 83339 and 83340 were completed on 9 and 10 November 1987. Interestingly, the higher chassis number was finished first, hence the lower registration number of E867 SAG that it acquired. Piggins and Rix ran a small fleet out of the Port of Montrose as an additional service to its main Stevedore activities. The haulage operation was run down over the years and ended up with just two trucks before being contracted out to a third party. *(Photo: Seddon Atkinson Historic Archive)*

This 4x2 T17 C32 unit was powered by the entry-level Cummins for the 4-11 chassis – a power unit that was also available in the 6x2 and 6x4 – which produced 308 bhp and was offered with the nine-speed Fuller RTX gearbox as standard, though the thirteen-speed RTO was available as an option. The 300–320 bhp sector was a hotly contested one at the end of the 1980s, the output range being well suited for UK 38-tonne operation. Although the Super E320 was at the lower end of output in terms of bhp, its large cubic capacity of 14 litres meant that plenty of torque was available, approximately 1,086 lb-ft at 1,200 rpm, which was more than a contemporary DAF 3600 and certainly enough for Interox's chemical movements at 38 tonnes.

(Photo: Seddon Atkinson Historic Archive)

I G Merrett was born out of the UK's post-war building boom, a time of plenty for haulage operators large and small. In its early years, the company used its ingenuity to adapt trucks to its own requirements, creating tractors from rigids and even building its own bodywork onto chassis. However, by the time this smart 4-11 joined the fleet in the late 1980s standard artics were the order of the day and Cummins was, perhaps, the engine of preference for

Merrett, with both this unit and a very similarly specified ERF E14 being so equipped. The company's work had also evolved to specialise in newsprint, confectionery and building materials.

Note the additional, circular side repeater indicator that the 4-11 gained on the front wing. However, the rectangular reflectors were fitted by the operator and not the factory. *(Photo: Adrian Cypher)*

With the industry's growing emphasis on aerodynamics and fuel efficiency, Seddon Atkinson developed this integrated roof spoiler and side screen system for the 4-11. The massive one-piece roof spoiler was open at the rear and was affixed to the roof via the clearly visible clips that locked it to the cab guttering. The item had an additional strip at the rear, which could be added or removed to suit a cab fitted with or without side screens. Les Sampson Services Ltd ran a fleet of around 50 trucks, mainly on container traffic. Although to ISO dimensions this highly unusual load was obviously something rather special and required this extending semi low-loader instead of the more normal skelly trailer. The company also ran a Seddon Atkinson franchise at one time. *(Photo: Seddon Atkinson Historic Archive)*

Hicks International was another company that enjoyed the distinction of operating the 400, 401 and 4-11 models over the years. This 4-11, judging by the special livery, was originally employed on the tomato distribution work that Hicks carried out for VHB, one of the UK's leading suppliers of tomatoes. It makes a fine sight as it bowls down the M4.

The unit was later put into the standard Hicks livery with the all-over white extending to the bumper, grille, front wings and sleeper windows. All tomato references were removed and the Hicks horseshoe and 'H' emblem was applied to the roof spoiler. Perhaps the later move to other traffic was dictated by the age of the unit and the perishable nature of the tomatoes. *(Photo: Marcus Lester)*

There would have been something hugely wrong if W & J Riding had not added the 4-11 to its large Seddon Atkinson fleet during the model's short production life, but add it, it did, and in impressive numbers, too.

The 4-11 was fitted with heated mirrors as standard, which were supplied in a three-mirror set-up that included a trailer swing mirror on the nearside. The effect of these, when combined with the new corner deflectors, was to virtually eliminate the old mirror fouling issue.

In the lower picture you will notice that the distinct 'A' logo was incorporated into the door handle. This was still the old International Harvester item, but with the 'IH' machined off and replaced with the 'A' logo.

Heated mirrors had been fitted to the 401 since 1985, but the revised door handle only appeared on the very last D-registered examples, probably as supply changed in readiness for the 4-11.

Note the fleet names, which Riding applied just below the front windows, 'Hal o' the Wynd' for E230 NFR and, rather appropriately for fleet No. 100, 'Centurion' for E170 MFV.

(Photos: Marcus Lester)

When the 4-11 was introduced, the limited availability of Gardner engines restricted availability for the 4-11 to just the 15.5-litre 6LYT, which, with two engines from Cummins and two from Rolls-Royce, left customers with a choice of five, covering 305–388 bhp. However, for the first time since 1975, all five engines were powerful enough to be listed for all chassis from the 4x2 to the 6x4. This situation was, perhaps, an early indicator of further rationalisation by Seddon Atkinson, which, with the introduction of the Strato range in 1988, would ultimately see the disappearance of Gardner engines altogether.

This nicely presented 4-11 of Maldwyn Davies makes a fine six-axle combination with this matching bulk tipper in tow. Note that the nice heated mirrors of the 4-11 have been changed for something simpler here.

[Photo: Adrian Cypher]

W & J Riding found its hand forced by the lack of its preferred power unit, the 6LXDT, in the 4-11 and instead purchased two early examples fitted with the larger 15.5-litre 6LYT. E600 DCK (chassis number 82339) was commonly thought to be the last 4-11 to leave the factory with this engine, but as production records show, another nine were completed afterwards, including Riding's own, E210 ERN (chassis number 82379), which was built and delivered in May 1987. In all, Seddon Atkinson fitted the 6LYT engine to 74 401/4-11 chassis between 1984 and 1988. The 6LYT was expensive and early units suffered from reliability issues, so it was no surprise when Seddon Atkinson, despite not listing it on spec sheets, reverted to fitting the 6LXDT in the 4-11 once the supply of that unit improved from the manufacturer.

Unlike all other Gardner engines fitted to the 401 and 4-11, the 6LYT demanded a nearside location for the snorkel airstack. *(Photo: Marcus Lester)*

The 4-11 was always going to be a stop-gap model, introduced to freshen up the five-year-old 401 and keep punters interested until the new Strato with the Cabtec cab was available. If Seddon Atkinson had worked to the same schedule as DAF and Pegaso, the Strato would have replaced the 4-11 after a year or so. As it was the 4-11 had to soldier on for nearer two years. Perhaps because of the impending release of the Strato, the 4-11 never had its own dedicated brochure printed; instead it made do with surreptitious appearances in Seddon Atkinson's 'Tractor' brochure, which also covered the 3-11. P M Rees and Sons ran 4-11s in 4x2 and 6x2 configurations on container and bulk powder work.

(Photo: Adrian Cypher)

The 4-11 interior was largely unchanged from that of the 401; however, it did benefit from a couple of small but significant tweaks. There was a new Bostrum Viking air suspension seat, which was actually first seen in the Silver Knight special editions and final 401s. The new design had thicker padding, was upholstered in a hard-wearing oatmeal fabric and the seat frame at the sides and rear was less exposed with the workings underneath now hidden behind a bellows-type moulding, all of which was easier to keep clean.

Also with driver comfort in mind, there was a new soft-touch steering wheel, with a distinct big 'A' logo horn push at its centre and spokes that were angled back to give a better view of the dashboard where the warning lights were now shrouded by a smoked black plastic cover, which made them unobtrusive until illuminated. The dashboard also featured some new grid-style graphics around the switches and heater controls and revised 'Seddon Atkinson' lettering applied to the fuse box lid. Lastly, a handy toolbox containing a bottle jack, wheel brace, etc., was developed for the passenger footwell. The clever design incorporated a sloping lid, which allowed the box to double as a convenient footrest. Incobulk was another contract that saw W & J Riding trucks painted in a customer livery.

(Photo: Marcus Lester)

The 4x2 and 6x2 general haulage layout was by far the most popular for 4-11 customers, but every now and then an operator with special requirements demanded the 6x4 chassis with the proven RA-472 rear bogie. This T24 C32 was one such example and was operated by a paper recycling company with this impressive compacting trailer, the front half of which telescoped into the rear section via hydraulic rams in between the trailer's chassis rails. The unit was completed on 5 October 1987 and delivered on 6 October with the chassis number 83083.

The generous air-gap between the cab and the new corner deflector is evident from this photograph. As well as creating a strong airstream to carry dirt away from the mirrors and windows, the new item improved ram air ventilation to such an extent that the old top window ventilators could be deleted and replaced with a fixed pane. *(Photo: Peter Davison)*

By the end of 4-11 production, the official engine choice was down to four. The last spec sheet for the model was published in May 1987 and listed the 6LYT, Super E320, 300Li and 340Li. Despite Perkins taking on the Rolls-Royce engine range and marketing them as Perkins Eagles, the spec sheets and model designations continued with the R suffix for Rolls-Royce; however, this was not the case for sales literature with brochures referring to Perkins Eagles. It was not until a Perkins engine was first fitted in a Strato chassis in 1989 that the R was dropped from the designation in favour of a P. The

slightly different nomenclature for a Strato so equipped being 17.33P. Despite only listing four engines, Seddon Atkinson was very open to 'special equipment' orders at the time and was happy to accommodate customers' wishes, where possible, to maintain sales. For example, if a 6LXDT was required, and one was actually available from Gardner, then an engineering release would be issued to replace all the 6LYT components with those for the 6LXDT on that particular chassis.

(Photo: Adrian Cypher)

Although largely anonymous and certainly plain, this late, post-August 1988 F-registration 4-11 was among the last of the 4-11s produced, which brought to a close 13 years of unbroken production since the first 400 appeared in 1975.

Towards the end of production, Seddon Atkinson started to list a Twin Splitter gearbox as an option over the standard nine-speed Fuller RTX. The Spicer gearbox was loved and hated by drivers in roughly equal amounts, but was to become the standard offering for the Strato.

In 1988 production shifted to the new model, which, equipped with the new Cabtec cab, made a technological jump over its predecessor similar to that made by the original 400 over the Borderer back in 1975.

Note the double-ended trailer of the type often used for long indivisible loads such as carpets.

(Photo: Adrian Cypher)

F33 RCW (chassis number 84683) originally left Oldham as a T17 C32 4x2 unit. The unit was built at the tail end of 4-11 production in June 1988 and delivered the following month. At some point in its career, the truck was altered, with a tag axle conversion, into a 6x2 format, and from the condition of the unit here it is reasonable to assume that this was done fairly early on. Whether this was in pursuit of the tax break that was available for six-axle truck/trailer combinations or to safeguard against axle overloading is not known. The compact wheelbase of the 4x2 4-11, like the 400 and 401 before, made it ideally suited to such conversions. The tell-tale sign of this unit's 4x2 origins is the full-length air stack and filter. All factory 6x2s and 6x4s featured a shorter stack, which allowed the filter canister to be mounted on a bracket above the height of the side rail to free up space on the chassis. *(Photo: Peter Davison)*

One of the last and possibly finest 4-11s was this example, beautifully turned out in the livery of R G Jellis & Son and obviously the pride and joy of its driver.

Despite its issues over the years – mainly concerning rust on the original 400 – the Motor Panels cab served Seddon Atkinson very well, especially as it was also the base for the 200 and 300 ranges, which would continue in production for a few more years. By 1988 it still offered a comfortable place to work and rest, but was now one of the oldest for a premium truck still in production. The design and engineering costs of a replacement would have spelled the end for a manufacturer of Seddon Atkinson's size, but, luckily its new parent company, ENASA of Spain, set up a deal with DAF to design and build the Cabtec cab, which would also be made available to Seddon Atkinson for its next heavy range.

Reg Jellis started his business in the 1950s with one vehicle and later became a stalwart of the preservation scene with a restored Bedford cattle truck. The Jellis fleet worked on bulk powder and was always impeccably turned out. The industry lost a true gentleman when Reg died.

Note the DAF 95 with Cabtec cab behind. *(Photo: Adrian Cypher)*

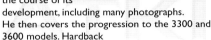